To the undiscovered stars.
To the people whose brilliance
the world has not yet seen,
but who know it is there.

Praise for Bill Hoogterp and his Own the Room training program

"Positive, fun, very professional, and efficient. . . . The surprise dividend was the morale and confidence boost—team building—for our group."
— JACK HAIRE
CEO of Parade Media Group

"Bill is probably the top speaking coach on the planet right now."
— MATTEO SCARAVELLI
vice president of corporate communications at Siemens

"The trainers make a compelling case for storytelling as a powerful form of communication in the board room. They taught us that by embracing our inner child (who always loved a great story), we can leave meaningful and lasting impressions as presenters."
— MELLODY HOBSON
president of Ariel Investments and
financial contributor to CBS News

"I highly recommend the Own the Room training."
— JACK GRIFFIN
CEO of Empirical Media and former CEO of Time, Inc.

"[Own the Room] did a training for some of our senior executives, and they said it was terrific. Every one of them came away with new insight and skills from the great training."
— STEPHEN FRIEDMAN
president of MTV

"In a word, Bill is amazing. His approach is simple, yet powerful. He helps you uncover your true voice in a powerful and dynamic way. I am forever grateful."
—KIM M. SHARAN
chief marketing officer and president of financial planning
and wealth strategies, Ameriprise Financial

"I learned more in three hours than I did in all my speaking courses combined."
—BRAD HAEBERLE
vice president at Siemens Building Technologies

"Bill is a genius. He simplifies the skills required to communicate effectively into manageable and understandable chunks. And he entertains throughout the experience!"
—STEVE ZALES
chief knowledge officer of Hudson

"Bill Hoogterp taught me to love my powerful voice and all of its inflection. Not only am I a better speaker after his training, but, just as importantly, I am a better listener."
—KELLY FLYNN
senior executive producer at CNN

"Bill can help anyone feel more comfortable and succeed at such an important skill."
—ELISABETH SHUE
Academy Award–nominated actress

"Bill Hoogterp has a great talent for demystifying the act of public speaking. His wisdom and expertise helped me to connect with an audience in a way I never had before and actually even enjoy it!"
—MOLLY RINGWALD
actress and author of *Getting the Pretty Back*
and *When It Happens to You*

"An exceptional and rewarding experience."
—RICHARD SCHIFF
Emmy Award–winning actor

"Sometimes in life, things are what they really say they are, and people actually do what they say they will do. No matter how many presentations or lectures you have done in the past, Own the Room will truly help you to see your audience in a completely different and most pleasing light. Bill will teach you *how* to own the room and take charge of your audience."
—DR. EDWIN MOSES
Olympic gold medalist, 400-meter hurdles

"Terrific and fun!"
—CELIA BOBROWSKY
director of community affairs at Major League Baseball

"Great training. Surprising how much you can learn with their approach."
—URBAN MEYER
head football coach at Ohio State University

"However good you think you are at public speaking, you will learn loads."
—DAVID RADFORD
group marketing director at CreativeLIVE

"I learned and saw how, with a few simple ideas and concepts, the same presentation can go from standard and ordinary to interesting and involving."
—JEFF KEANE
cartoonist for *The Family Circus*

Your Perfect Presentation

Speak in Front of Any Audience
Anytime Anywhere and
Never Be Nervous Again

BILL HOOGTERP

NEW YORK   CHICAGO   SAN FRANCISCO
ATHENS   LONDON   MADRID
MEXICO CITY   MILAN   NEW DELHI
SINGAPORE   SYDNEY   TORONTO

2 3 4 5 6 7 8 9 0   QFR/QFR   1 2 0 9 8 7 6 5 4

ISBN 978-0-07-182500-9
MHID   0-07-182500-2

e-ISBN 978-0-07-182501-6
e-MHID   0-07-182501-0

Library of Congress Cataloging-in-Publication Data

Hoogterp, Bill.
  Your perfect presentation : speak in front of any audience anytime anywhere and never be nervous again / Bill Hoogterp.
    pages cm
  ISBN-13: 978-0-07-182500-9 (alk. paper)
  ISBN-10: 0-07-182500-2 (alk. paper)
  1. Public speaking. 2. Business presentations. I. Title.
  PN4192.B87H66 2014
  808.5'1—dc23

                                                          2013045561

Own the Room® is a registered trademark of Blue Planet Training, LLC.

McGraw-Hill Education books are available at special quantity discounts to use as premiums and sales promotions or for use in corporate training programs. To contact a representative, please visit the Contact Us pages at www.mhprofessional.com.

Contents

★

v

PART III

MAKING THE *AUDIENCE* THE STAR

PART IV

THE WHOLE WORLD IS A STAGE

Foreword

★

Who is this guy? That was my reaction when I first saw the reserved and mysterious Bill Hoogterp in action in June 2010. I had just become editor of *Parade* magazine and was in Washington, DC, to introduce the very first Parade All-American Service Team to Vice President Joe Biden. Because Bill had played a role in helping to create the program and select the team, he was there at the Washington headquarters of Points of Light to congratulate the winners. I had been told that he was going to coach the kids on their big meet and greet. That afternoon, I learned that Bill was a cofounder of CafeMom as well as a leadership coach, but to be honest, I found it hard to pinpoint what exactly he did—never mind how he was going to prep so many kids in such a short amount of time.

The service team was a group of 15 kids from all across America. What they had in common were clever, innovative ideas for changing their schools, their neighborhoods, and their country. Some of them were precocious and very capable of handling themselves around adults. But most were gawky, self-conscious, and feeling a bit lost in their surroundings. Bill sat in the middle of the room as the kids shuffled into chairs, looking a little out of place around the big conference table. We went around the room and introduced ourselves. The kids rambled on. Some of them barely got above a whisper. Others failed to make eye contact. They were kids, after all. But their ideas had so much potential, and the fact that they didn't quite know how to deliver them in a sound bite was heartbreaking. After a while, Bill adjourned the meeting and took the kids off to work with them for an hour.

The next day, the service team arrived at the White House to make the presentations. A few of the girls ran into Elena Kagan, who was in the midst of Supreme Court confirmation preparations, in the ladies' room. It was a heady experience, with Vice President Biden there to salute the kids and their work, so it was hard to imagine the day getting any better. Then it did: When each child stood up to share what he or she had done, that child spoke with wit and clarity. All the children's voices were strong. They smiled. They told stories. They connected. It was as if Tinker Bell had flicked her wand and showered public speaking pixie dust on this crew. I looked around to find Bill to congratulate him on this miraculous transformation, but was told that he had left. Poof. He was gone.

Luckily for me, Bill quickly reappeared in my life. He invited me to a seminar, and before I knew it, I was using a prop, modulating my voice, moving around the room, and "getting over myself." As an editor at Time, Inc., I had taken my share of public speaking and presentation courses, but I had never experienced anything like the lively, engaging, and fun afternoon that I spent with Bill and his merry band of coaches. That's when it dawned on me that Own the Room was not your average public speaking course. Sure, I had learned some surefire ways to connect with a crowd, but it was how I felt when I was doing it—alive, confident, and unembarrassed—that really stood out for me. I felt like myself in front of a crowd. I heard my voice. What a powerful moment to experience. What a magical thing to feel.

Today, whenever I see anyone give a speech, I think of Bill. Did the person start with a question or a prop? How quickly are my filters going up? I now know that a good speaker can command both my head and my heart—if that speaker uses the right techniques. And when the speaker is so-so? I wonder what Bill's coaches could do for him or her. I wish Bill's class could be a mandatory part of childhood (and teacher) education because of the power it unlocks in young minds. I know Bill's book will be a must-have reference for anyone who wants to be a better leader in any business. And I believe that Own the Room will be your ticket to own whatever room you're in. The fun starts now.

MAGGIE MURPHY

Editor in Chief, *Parade*

Preface

★

The concept of *perfect* is powerful, yet it is dangerous out of context. Context matters.

Do you know what an IQ test is? Most of us do. But have you ever heard of a CQ test? A CQ test measures your creativity quotient. There is no agreed-upon CQ in the scientific sense, but the research produces some interesting insights.

In one iteration, a CQ test was given to very young children, around four years old, and most of them scored very high. The same test given to ten-year-olds resulted in much lower scores. This was shocking to the researchers until they considered one key factor: what happens between the ages of four and ten?

School.

Before we go to school, questions can have many answers. If you color the tree orange, everyone thinks it's beautiful. No matter how you sing a song, everyone thinks it's cute.

Then you go to school and learn that there is only one right answer to most questions:

1 + 1 = 2, and every other answer is *wrong*.

C-A-T spells cat, and every other spelling is *wrong*.

In math and in spelling, there usually is only one correct answer, but this lesson spills over into other aspects of our life. We grow up applying this lens to other areas.

Wait a minute, if our religion is right, then all the other ones must be . . .

If these faces on the magazine covers are beautiful, then the rest of us who don't look like that must be . . .

If ours is a great country, then the other ones must be . . .

The idea that there is only *one* right answer is the taproot of a dangerous mindset. And it's a false concept. It's just not true. There can be more than one right answer to certain life questions (and plenty of wrong answers, too).

It makes sense for teachers to stress the importance of right answers for math and spelling, because those subjects require precision. Great teachers, however, help students to understand, just as importantly, that there can be many right answers to *most other* questions.

What's the point?

Don't answer the wrong questions in life. If you can, look around or outside and see if you spot a tree. Now, answer this next question quickly, without thinking: Is that tree perfect?

I have asked many people this question, and the knee-jerk reaction is almost always, "No."

So I ask, "Then should we cut it down?"

They say, "Of course not."

"Then should we fix it?"

"*Of course not.* That's ridiculous!"

"But you said it's not perfect."

"*Is the tree perfect?*" is *not* the right question. That is *not* how you evaluate a tree. What are some *right* or better questions for evaluating a tree?

Is it alive?

Is it growing?

Does it bear fruit or give shade?

Is it beautiful?

These are all better questions for evaluating a tree.

A lot of times people get stuck because they are trying to come up with the right answer to a wrong question. Don't answer the wrong questions in life.

I want you to answer this next question again, quickly and without thinking.

Are *you* perfect?

If you answered, "No," put your left hand out and gently spank it with your right. You fell into the trap. You answered a *wrong* question! You can't evaluate yourself or any person that way. We are not math equations or phonic products. How do you evaluate a person? (*Hint:* We share a lot in common with trees.)

Are we alive? Are we growing? Are we bearing fruit? Are we beautiful?

Okay, Bill, that's a nice philosophical discussion. Let's continue it over a favorite beverage, but what has this got to do with presentations?

I have seen person after person get stuck on this concept of "perfect." It's hard for you to move forward and grow because you are stuck on the setting that you are not good or perfect now. It's like trying to drive a Ferrari with the parking brake on. So many people let this concept hold back their power.

Now, are your *presentations* perfect?

Ah . . . you didn't fall into the trap this time. Nice.

Your beauty and power are derived from making your presentations come to life and watching your ability grow. You can watch a tree all day, but can you ever actually see it grow? And yet they all do. So do we.

Did I connect with my audience? Was I memorable? These are the *right* questions for evaluating your presentations, and they will help you to enjoy the process of reaching your own potential.

Let's grow. You can just read the book, or you can create the conditions to blossom and be beautiful and confident. After all, you are perfect at being you.

Acknowledgments

★

This book would not have been possible without Elizabeth Kravitz, Casey Ebro, and the inspiration, support, and assistance of the following: Andre Agassi, Dave Allan, John Amos, Syd Atlas, Diana Aviv, Dave Barger, Birgit Bassarak, Chris Baumann, Doug Becker, Jill Bernardes, Anouche Billet, Christian Bindl, Cory Booker, Raheem Booker, Mike Buckley, Jeffrey Bundy, Stephen Burwell, Sylvia Mathews Burwell, Dave Burwick, Jeb Bush, Alex Byrd, Ian Cameron, Penny & Jon Carolin, Ben Casnocha, Ray Chambers, Bettina Cisneros, Kim Crain, Emmanuel Delgado, Emiliano Diez, Chris Dinkel, Tuyet Dorr, David Drake, Arne Duncan, Leo Ehrline, Craig Faller, Corey Fenstemacher, Allan Fisher, Karen Fitzgerald, Kelly Flynn, Stephen Friedman, Himanshu Garg, Florencia Garrido, Melissa Gerr, Panio Gianopoulis, Icema Gibbs, Christine and Michael Gilfillan, Evie Goldfine, Andreas Graf, Grant Greenberg, Harald Griem, Jack Haire, Vanessa Harris, Susan Hassan, Geri Hazelitt, Sarah Herringer, Mellody Hobson, Stuart Hockridge, Reid Hoffman, Bill and Judy Hoogterp, Brett Hoogterp, Paul Hoogterp, Dave Hopping, Beverly Horowitz, Desmond Howard, Susan Howie, Arianna Huffington, Beth Hurvitz, Joichi Ito, Javier Jaime, Tony Kaperick, Joel Kaplan, Bob Kermanshahi, Wendy Kopp, Martha Kramer, Stefanie Krauth, Mercedes Kuilan, Stephen Kutz, Chad Laws, Diane Ledesma, Michelle Kydd Lee, Rachel Long, Anthony Lopez, Charlie Lowrey, Helmuth Ludwig, Jessica Maarek, George Markantonis, Fusako Matsui, Joe Mayock, John McArthur, Cherita Mcintye, Rita Menz, Urban Meyer,

Kathy Mitchell, Darshna Modi, Brigitte Mohn, Chris Mortell, Maggie Murphy, Beth Nickels, Dan Nova, Michelle Nunn, Nkem Nwuneli, John Oroho, Chris Park, Reimar Paschke, Michelle Peluso, Ethan Penner, Jorge Perez, Angelika Peters, Pam Piro, Manoue Poirier, John Porter, Roberto Pradilla, Andrea Prehofer, German Ramirez, Joe Ricci, Mickie Rinehart, Molly Ringwald, Michael Sanchez, Sheryl Sandberg, Tim Scanlan, Matteo Scaravelli, Richard Schiff, Jacob Schimmel, Elliot Schrage, Tom Scott, Nikki Shapiro, Kim Sharan, Bob Shephard, Erick Shepherd, Wendy Shepherd, David Shin, Andrew Shue, Eric Spiegel, Ted Spritzer, Ingrid Stransky, Martin Stumbillig, Etienne Szivo, Dieter Troller, Lisa Utzschneider, Peter Vincent, Nina Volpe, Jimmy Wales, George Walker, Rhonda Walton, Casey Wasserman, Paula Weiner, Ann Weinerman, Richard Whitten, Judee Ann Williams, Andrea Wishom, Achim Wolter, Matt Yale, Amie Yavor, and Alp Yoruk.

On behalf of Maria and I, special thanks to Roberto Pradilla, Dolly Wen, Michael Balaoing, Mikkel Kloster, and Stephanie Geffner. Also to Chris Hattersley, Rachel Warner, Melanie Tolomeo, and Cassandra Farmer. And to my book collaborator, Robin Wallace, and Dmitriy Guzner, who provided the art.

PART I

HOW THE
STAGE WORKS

The basic building blocks of theory for star speakers are:

★ Understanding the brain: how filters, pictures, emotions, and mirror neurons work

★ Converting nervousness into fun

★ Getting over yourself

★ Being memorable

★ Eliminating weak language and developing strong language

★ Harnessing feedback and video

CHAPTER 1

It's All About You, When You Are the Audience

Tell me and I forget. Teach me and I remember.
Involve me and I learn.
—Benjamin Franklin

Read the following words out loud:

Softly

Quickly

Slowly

Energy

Now, read them again, but this time, pronounce the word, as the word. Harmonize the tone of your voice with the meaning of the word. If you are feeling Zen, *become* the word as you say it.

softly

QUICKLY

s...l...o...w...l...y

ENERGY!

I'm known among my friends and colleagues as "Bill, who has a quirky ability to make anyone a better public speaker and presenter." I do this through a training system that I and others developed called Own the Room®. Our system helps people find the star speaker that's hiding inside of them, and some pretty big and cool companies and a growing number of famous people and leaders from all walks of life have hired our coaches to do just that.

Converting our system into book form was a challenge, because at Own the Room trainings, we're all about fun—games, drills, exercises, laughter, and constant practice and feedback both from a live audience and through various video technologies. So, if this book seems a little unusual to you as you read it—and it will—it's because we want to re-create the transformative experience of a live training for you so that you can improve as quickly as our students do.

Which returns us to our opening exercise. What did you notice? How did you feel experimenting with your voice?

Modulating your voice is a super-simple technique you can use to excite an audience. Most speakers will just get loud to convey their enthusiasm—and that can definitely help you excite your audience. But, the secret to great speaking is to release yourself to your content. Let the words tell *you* how they should be delivered, and release your voice range into your content.

If you and I were together in person, I would already have had you speaking on camera three or four times in the few minutes you've just spent reading this book. And, I promise you, you will be doing tons of exercises and skill-building drills, including video-taping yourself, as you read the book. Still, I must warn you, that the first few chapters are mostly theory. I couldn't help it. You need to build a foundation, a stage to stand on, in order to become a terrific presenter in your own style. If you'll stick with me through some theory, once you build your foundation, the skill building will move much faster.

This book is about *you*. *You* are the central character here; *you* are the hero. You can be a good, very good, or even superstar speaker. How good you become depends on *you*. Can you do it just by reading this book? Yes, but you have to make a choice. All heroes have to make choices.

Have you seen the original *Karate Kid* movie? Daniel decides to perform the "wax on, wax off" task given him by Mr. Miyagi, and great things happen for him that would not have happened had he dismissed the instruction as unimportant or refused to do it.

Make your choice a clear and conscious one. Take your right hand, raise it up high, and imagine that it is the top of a mountain, a symbol of you as an amazing speaker and presenter—your potential. In any room, meeting, or conversation, you are awesome whenever you want to be, and people hang on your every word. Your right hand is where you want to *go*.

Now, with your left hand, show how high up the mountain you are *now*. The very bottom is where you started; you have already made a lot of progress, but you want to get to your top. So, put your left hand at where you are *now*.

The only way up the mountain is to climb—to step and stumble, and to be breathless at times. There are no escalators on the mountain of life. When you are out of your comfort zone, *that* is when you are growing. We provide steps to make it easier and handrails to hold on to when you need them, but only you can put one foot in front of the other.

The reward for all that work is how great you will feel and a skill that you will enjoy for life and that may enable you to help others more than you know.

The path up the mountain involves many, many steps. These include the practice tasks and exercises in this book. Of course, you *could* just read the book and skip the exercises—and if you do, you will find that at the end, you have a much better understanding of various public speaking and communication dynamics. But you won't be much higher up the mountain.

I have had the honor of training many amazing people: those who were nervous and now aren't; those who were verbose but now are powerfully concise; those from all walks of life who can now present confidently on almost any topic, but especially in their areas of expertise.

It all starts with a simple choice. Your choice now, hero, is to say, "I want to get there, and I *will* do some exercises, so give me the bunny trail, not too hard." Some of these exercises are serious and some are silly, but there is a method to the madness, and they work in concert to get you up higher quickly.

Or you can say, "I want the diamond trail, the hardest path. Whatever exercises you give me, I will do more!"

But first, let's have you take a step away from base camp with your first exercise and see if you actually do it.

When you read the word *BEGIN* in all caps, take a little cup or bottle of water in one hand and pour just a little of it into the other hand. Hold the water for a minute, trying not to spill any of it, while you think about why you want to be a great speaker. Let me repeat this, because how good a speaker you become depends on this unusual task.

When you read the word *BEGIN*, put down this book, pour a little water from one hand into the other, and hold it for a minute, as long as you can, without spilling any. As you do this, think of why you want to be a great presenter.

"C'mon, Bill, this is silly. Do you really expect me to do this?"

Okay, first of all, the goal is not to make you feel silly. If you feel silly, that is just a bonus for the universe—and if you are reading this on a plane and someone sitting next to you thinks you're crazy, you get double bonus points. This is the first, and arguably the most important, test of the whole book.

I want you to reread the paragraphs describing the task as many times as you need to do to make sure you understand the exercise. Now, moment of truth. Ready?

BEGIN.

If you did the task, nice job! You are in "attack" learning mode with a "fearless learner" mindset. You took not only a big step, but a leap of faith. Let's get to work.

If you didn't do the task, you are in "passive" reading mode. There's nothing wrong with that; it's the norm for how we read books, so that response is completely understandable. But if that's the case, I cannot unlock your potential. You might as well return the book for a refund or pass it on to someone else. I don't want to sound harsh, but your time is your most precious asset. You are generous with your time, but I am protective of it. The distinction between a passive setting and an attack setting matters.

All the great speakers were bad speakers at first.
—RALPH WALDO EMERSON

Fifty years ago, researchers at Stanford University conducted studies on delayed gratification in which children were offered one marshmallow immediately, but a second marshmallow if they could wait for the scientist to leave the room and return 15 minutes later before eating the first one. These studies, known collectively as the "marshmallow experiment," concluded that the children who were able to delay gratification had better outcomes in life, based on a range of criteria.

Just as in the marshmallow studies, your default setting can have an enormous impact on your life over time. I have trained a lot of great presenters in the world—from CEOs to celebrities—and it all starts with a choice. I need you, *on purpose*, to choose a setting for yourself for reading this book. The way you choose that setting is by pouring the water.

Passive means that you will "rent" some content knowledge and not gain much skill.

Attack means that you will actively participate and watch yourself gradually develop a new set of powerful skills that you will enjoy for the rest of your life.

If you didn't do the task before, get some water and do it now! Click into attack mode. Welcome to the fast lane, baby! Now, towel off. We'll wait. You are worth the wait.

Now that you have toweled off—and for the rest of the book—I will be assuming that you're in attack mode and will perform the tasks. To quote the great and wise Yoda, "There is only do and not do." My promise to you (and you can see from testimonials how well our system works) is that there is nothing in this book that does not have a purpose. It will all make sense in the end.

If, in the course of reading this book, you skip an exercise or two, go back and do them. No excuses.

What is the point of the water?

After we've attended a meeting or a presentation, we forget most of what we just heard the minute we walk out. It slips from our minds like water through our fingers. People sometimes introduce me as an expert, but when it comes to communication, I'd say that we are all experts and all learners. And as learners, we cannot hold on to the water unless we have a vessel, a glass. For you to "hold" the lessons of this book, to truly learn them so that you can reach your maximum potential, the glass is *action*. The exercises represent that action—the glass in which you will hold the lessons that will transform you into a great speaker. The action deepens the learning and makes it last.

Grab a pen and get ready to write in the margin of this book. (Go ahead and scribble a lot, so the book will look as if it was attacked.) Now, think of all of the meetings you have ever attended in your whole life. All of the meetings . . . of . . . your . . . *whole . . . life*. Whatever the purpose and whoever was running the meetings, you were in the room. If you added them all up and averaged them together, how would you rank their efficiency? Using a scale from 0 to 100—where 100 indicates that every minute of every one of those meetings brought us to nirvana and solved all the world's problems, and 0 means that every minute was a complete waste of time—rate those meetings. Be brutally honest. Now write that number here _____ or in the margin of this book.

At the in-person Own the Room trainings we do around the world, we always start with this question about meeting efficiency.

Can you guess our worldwide average?

It's 37 percent.

So, there was 63 percent inefficiency.

If you got home from work tonight and discovered that 37 percent of the water from your kitchen faucet was coming out the right way, but 63 percent was spraying all over the place, what would you do? If you are handy, you'd get out your toolbox and fix it. Those of us who can barely change a lightbulb (like me) would call a plumber.

If you went to bed with $100 in your wallet, but found that you had only $37 left when you woke up, what would you be? Married. Just kidding.

If 63 percent of your work profits were being wasted with no obvious benefit, would that be acceptable to you? So why do you tolerate 63 percent of your time being wasted?

In our in-person trainings, we spend very little time listening to lectures or in classroom-type instruction. We spend almost no time reading. There's a tip or a technique, and then a quick practice. We do an exercise on camera and play it back. Another tip, and then more practice. A game and some laughter. We are replicating that process here to deliver the same learning experience through this book. So, has the knowledge that 63 percent of your time is being wasted motivated you to commit to improving your communication skills?

Great! Now that we've got you committed, let's talk about *you*.

Using your fingers, answer the following three questions:

1. How much do you like speaking in public?

   On a scale of zero to ten—with ten meaning, "That is my favorite thing in the world; how did you know?" and zero meaning, "Yuck; I hate speaking to groups, especially big ones"—show me with your fingers how much you enjoy public speaking. Put up your fingers. Now, write that number here: _____

   If your number is high, excellent! You already know how it feels to make a group laugh, feel, learn, or grow. You are about to like it even more.

   If your number is low, that's even better! You are . . . normal. A British magazine did a survey of Americans' fears, and guess what our number one fear was? You guessed it, public speaking. Know what was number two? Death. Yes, I am sure spiders was on there somewhere, but death was number two.*

---

*Findings from a 1973 survey by the *Sunday London Times* that were later published in David Wallechinsky, Irving Wallace, and Amy Wallace, *The Book of Lists* (New York: William Morrow & Co., 1977). This has been the subject of much debate. According to the National Institutes of Health, 74 percent of Americans suffer from a fear of public speaking.

We are more afraid of speaking in public than we are of dying. The great comedian Jerry Seinfeld makes the best joke about this. He says, "Does that seem right? That means when we go to the funeral, we would rather be the one lying in the box . . . than the one delivering the eulogy."

Okay, next question.

2. How good are you now?

Using your fingers and the same zero-to-ten scale as before, if you were to rate your current communication skills, how good would you say you are now? For this question, I want you to think of all your communications—how you perform in front of small groups, in front of big groups, and even one-on-one—and average them. A score of ten means that you are better than Bill Clinton and Ronald Reagan combined; zero means that you can't communicate at all, to anyone—and you don't really get what's so funny about the Seinfeld joke.

It's hard to be objective about ourselves. *Hmm, how good am I really?* Put up your fingers. Now, go ahead and write the number here: ___

Now that you've assessed both your fears and your abilities as a speaker, it's time to assess your goals.

3. How good a speaker do you want to be?

Oh, well, I'm reading a book on presenting, so I have to say, "Ten."

Well, there are no tens. We all have something to teach, but we also have much we can learn. So no tens, but be honest. If you've rated yourself a four, you are happy being a four, and all is in harmony, then answer, "Four." You have to own how much you want to improve and why, or the process toward improvement won't begin. It helps to set a specific goal for what you want to accomplish; then we can help you grow your "irrational commitment" to your goals.

So really give it some thought. How great a speaker do you truly want to become? Put up your fingers. Go ahead and write the number here: ___

And now for the big question. No fingers this time.

4. Why do you want to improve your public speaking skills?

Why do you really want to improve? Again, let's mix it all together: speaking to big groups, to small groups, one-on-one—all formats. You can't become great unless you want to, and unless you have a reason that will motivate you to get there.

Why do you want to get better?

Whenever we ask this question at our training sessions, the answers are many and varied. Here are some common responses. Circle any that are close to yours and/or add your own:

Oh, good for my job.

Important for my career.

I want to get my message across.

I really want to be more effective.

I just like it.

I hate being afraid.

Other: _____.

Do you notice any similarities among these answers?

Are you familiar with the intellectual to emotional change chart?

**Intellectual
(I should)**

These answers all represent an intellectual response, what we at Own the Room call "intellectual inflection." Whenever we want to change something in our lives—*I want to learn Spanish* or *I want to quit smoking*—we start from a point called the *intellectual inflection* point. It's when our brain is telling us, "I should do that."

What usually happens? It doesn't work. We fall back into the same habits.

I should exercise every day. I want to, but I don't.

Sometimes, that is where our motivation ends, and the change we are seeking never takes place. Intellec-

tual motivation is usually just not strong enough to trigger that change.

We need to reach what we call the *emotional inflection* point.

I was out of breath walking up two flights of stairs when the elevator was out of order. I am going to join the gym after work.

This is when change happens.

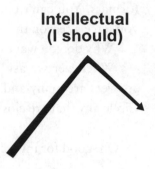

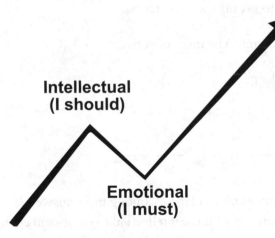

Most decisions, even in business, are made when the *emotional trigger* is pulled. This doesn't mean that there is no intellect or logic involved. Intellect and logic often form the basis of our decisions, but the trigger for becoming "irrationally committed" to a goal is emotional.

Think of some of the changes you have made in your life—big and small, positive and negative, professional and personal. For a while, you probably said, "I should, I should." Then something triggered the emotional inflection that you needed, and you made the change happen.

Now let's return to the reasons we gave for wanting to improve. Are these first few answers intellectual or emotional?

Oh, good for my job.

Important for my career.

I want to get my message across.

I really want to be more effective.

Correct, they're intellectual. Are they powerful enough to trigger the change?

No, they are not. We need to get you down to the bottom of the chart, the emotional trigger. Let's get to the good stuff.

I want to really impress people.

I want people to respect me.

I want to command a room.

I want to be remembered.

I want to not be nervous—or afraid!

These are all normal, healthy, and natural emotional responses.

When we start from a point of intellectual inflection, our ability to change plummets immediately and sharply. It's just not enough of a motivator to keep us going.

Emotional inflection, however, triggers change. It is at the point of emotional inflection that we throw a switch in our brains and decide that we are going to make it happen.

Authors Dan and Chip Heath address the difference between our emotional and intellectual motivations for change in their book *Switch: How to Change Things When Change Is Hard.*

They compare our emotional side to an elephant, and our rational side to someone riding the elephant. Should the six-ton elephant and the rider ever disagree on which direction to go, they write, the rider is going to lose every time. The rider is completely overmatched.

So reach into your brain right now and flip the emotional switch.

Emotional inflection can result from a positive or a negative emotion. Either one works. Positive emotional triggers are the desire or motivation to want to make a group laugh or learn something. *I want them to remember me, and be impressed!* When you can make a group laugh or learn something, it's a rush, like a little drug. I want you to feel the effects of this "good" drug. And you will, whenever you want to, when your presentations bring more value to others.

On the other hand, are you sick and tired of staying in the office so late, knowing that you're stuck there because of lost productivity and inefficiencies throughout the day? Does 63 percent inefficiency—your time being wasted—make you angry enough to change? What would it be worth to you to get out of work 30 minutes earlier for the rest of your life because you improved your efficiency some during the day?

This is an example of a negative emotional trigger. It's possible for you to fix all of those problems during your workday, but only if you emotionally decide to make it happen and throw that switch in your mind.

To reach the point of emotional inflection, you must consider carefully, and figure out, why you want to become a better speaker. A good car mechanic understands why an engine works. A great coach understands why athletes are driven to compete. Little by little, page by page, you will, yourself, become a professional speaking coach, with yourself as your number one client. If you can internalize the "what, why, and how" of your desire to become a better speaker, the results will come along for the ride.

You may be wondering how I came to know all of this or why you should listen to me. Personally, I don't think you're wondering that at all. Knowing my story won't help you improve any faster. But, my editor says you're not going to pay much attention to me unless I tell you about my background and how I developed my public speaking expertise. Fortunately, I have surrounded myself with people, such as my editor, who are much smarter than me, and I have noticed that they have this remarkable ability to be right about things when I am forced to listen to them. However, you have my permission to skip the next few paragraphs and jump to the good stuff.

When I was in my early twenties, I spent several months traveling across the United States (from Harvard to UCLA), working with some wonderful nonprofit groups and colleagues, and presenting every day on the topics of community service, hunger, and homelessness. One day, I decided to step back and do what you are doing right now. I asked myself, "How good a speaker am I, actually?"

It's hard to be objective about yourself, I suppose, but I determined that on a scale of zero to ten, I was about a four. Not bad, but not good either.

My other insight was recognizing that I wasn't getting better the more I spoke, I was just becoming more *comfortable* with my habits. I decided that I wanted to become *good*, and I started devising my own techniques for becoming a better presenter. I never attended a training course or read a book on presentations. I know that there is a trove of great material out there. But when I was creating my own techniques, I was a little afraid that if I learned other people's secrets, I wouldn't be able to unlearn them. You can't unring a bell, and I didn't want to subconsciously steal other people's material. Even so, I have learned a great deal from others. Pretty much anything I say that sounds remotely intelligent, I promise I learned from someone else. Anything that makes no sense at all, that's the stuff I made up myself.

Because of the frequency of my near-daily talks on campuses and at conferences, I was able to invent, try, and tweak new techniques rapidly. In Michigan, where I grew up, there's an expression: "Even a blind squirrel gets a nut once in a while." I don't think I have a great voice or even that much aptitude or charisma, but I made up for it with persistence. I was always trying new things. (Even now, it sometimes drives my tech team and my assistants crazy because I will make up things on the spot. It keeps them on their toes!) I started to really improve. I earned $100 for my first paid speech. I was so excited! As my speaking skill grew from a four to a five, and then to a six and a seven, so did my impact. As the months passed, I got paid $200 per speech, then $500, then $1,000. One of the high points of that time was being invited to be the commencement speaker at Foothill College in California. They said I was certainly the youngest commencement speaker they'd ever had, and the only one who wore tennis shoes. (I wasn't making a statement; they were the only shoes I had. In my defense, they were pretty cool shoes.) A year later, Bill Gates paid me $3,000 *not to speak*, but that's another story. It was a rush to be able to move an audience, to make them laugh or teach them something. I was hooked on public speaking.

My professional path changed when my great friend Jim Mustacchia invited me to help him give a leadership training program in Germany. Jim is a brilliant executive trainer, and he lured me with the promise of a few hours with his clients at a luxurious resort in Germany. After a 12-hour day, then a 3-hour dinner with his clients, I was hooked again, but this time not on the "doing" but on the teaching of

What do former British prime minister Winston Churchill and Hollywood icon Marilyn Monroe have in common?

They both stuttered. In Churchill's case, he also spoke with a lisp. Yet Marilyn Monroe became one of the most famous actresses of all time, and Churchill is regarded as one of history's great orators and political leaders.

What did Churchill have in common with another legendary orator and leader, the civil rights activist Martin Luther King Jr.?

Both men were known to practice their speaking and rehearse their speeches over and over again before delivering them to the public. Churchill, in fact, memorized his speeches forward and backward. Both Winston Churchill and Dr. King were charged with the daunting task of motivating people and inspiring them to action—to herculean action—during extremely difficult times. Imagine if either had failed to recognize how crucial his public speaking skills were to his accomplishing the task at hand.

others: how they can do it; how *they* can be the star. I was foolishly invited back again, and I collaborated with Jim on the great work he was doing in leadership development.

Eventually, my wife, Maria, and I decided to start our own firm, Blue Planet Training. All the techniques I had developed for myself now had a new purpose, but they needed to be tweaked and expanded into a system that could be taught to others—a system that could be learned quickly and deeply, so that others could become terrific presenters. The Own the Room methodology began to develop. That was a few years ago, and thanks to many wonderful people, it has been growing rapidly ever since.

SUMMARY

★ Flip your switch to *attack mode*. When an emotional trigger motivates us to improve ourselves, our potential is limitless.

CHAPTER 2

From Nervousness to Fun

★

We don't cure fear. We convert it. Your nervousness doesn't go away. It turns into enjoyment. The intensity of how much some people didn't like it before is how much they like it once they understand. It is so cool to watch.
—Roberto Pradilla, COO, Own the Room

Take out your smartphone or tablet and do a super-simple exercise. Go to the camera, click on video, and reverse the lens to show your beautiful face. Record yourself pointing to your face on camera and saying, "Wow, this face is *so* attractive." (*Bill, do I really have to say that? Yes.*) Then play it back and notice at least one thing that you did well. Then delete the evidence. Make sure to click on the trash can, not the YouTube button. (If you do post it on YouTube by mistake, I cannot be held responsible, but send me the link so that I can see it!)

Throughout my career as a presenting, communication, and public speaking coach, I've worked with corporate executives, business owners, entrepreneurs, celebrities, and politicians, and not once have I conducted a training session during which the issue of nervousness and fear has not come up, usually as a primary concern. While it is not an issue at all for many people, you'd be shocked at how many terrific, very famous, and very successful people—even those who make their living in the public eye—are extremely uncomfortable about speaking in public in certain circumstances. Overcoming this is simple.

"That's easy for you to say, Bill."

It is.

What you *think* of as nervousness is really just trapped energy. Once you see and understand that, it is a simple thing to fix, but before we get to that, let me give you a choice: Do you want to learn techniques for overcoming nervousness after it's happened? Or do you want a shortcut to never being nervous in the first place, but it's a harsh truth?

Shortcut?

Own the Room coaches have shared this with many executives, CEOs, and celebrities around the world, and many have come back to us to tell us that it really works.

"When I finally internalized that short sentence, I actually stopped getting nervous. Wow."

The harsh truth is this:

Get over yourself.

Forget yourself. The speaker *doesn't* matter. Your magic happens when you focus on how to get your *audience* to know something and do something. To *feel* something, as one of the top coaches, Michael Balaoing, says so well. When you stop thinking that it's about you, that is when your greatness begins to emerge. It's about the audience getting your content.

When we focus on ourselves, we create a barrier—a filter—between ourselves and the audience. Because we are trying to avoid making mistakes, we have put up our guard to protect ourselves. Our guard is our own filter. You know what happens when we put up our filter? Those in our audience mirror us and put up their filter. Now we have *double*-blocked ourselves from the audience.

That's no good. Not to sound too Zen about it, but when we try to send our energy out toward the audience, it instead bounces back off our own filter, creating that paralyzing feeling. The portion that manages to get through our filter bounces off *their* filter, their shield. Not much is getting through.

When we lower our own filter, those in the audience will lower theirs, and the energy can flow back and forth between you and your audience.

There are many trainers and companies in this field. The vast majority of them are quite good and *very* effective—and they're smart and interesting people to boot! There is also no question but that all our programs share certain similarities, because none of us is "inventing" so much as we are all *discovering* what works and why—though we may teach it in different ways and with our own personality. And one thing that all great trainers know is that focusing on fear—what is perceived as "just fear"—is counterproductive. I will focus this chapter on it, to help you see it differently.

What you think of as fear is not really fear at all. All your efforts to use your willpower to overcome your fears will not work, because fear is not the problem. How many times have you tried *to will* yourself not to be afraid? How well has that worked?

I am not saying that fear doesn't exist. I am not being that existential. But the dread or anxiety that you may associate with speaking in front of a group of people is not fear. You know what your real problem is in this case? We helped an executive named Paula figure it out on her own.

Paula: I understand everything about getting over myself, but I still get so nervous.

Coach: You know what your problem is?

Paula: What?

Coach: You care. You actually care. Don't you?

Paula: *(nods)*

Coach: More specifically, and tell me if I got these right, you care about doing a good job.

Paula: Yes.

Coach: You care about the audience.

Paula: Yeah.

Coach: You care about your content.

Paula: *(nods)*

Coach: And you care about how you are *perceived.*

Paula: Yes.

The first three types of caring are strengths. The fourth one—caring about how your audience perceives *you*—wipes out the other three.

$$\text{Comfort} = \frac{\text{Content} + \text{Audience} + \text{Performance}}{\text{Self-Perception}}$$

I was coaching a guy, the CEO of a company in Silicon Valley, who had what he thought was a paralyzing fear of public speaking. Now he doesn't, and he really enjoys presenting. What changed? Here is part of a conversation I had with him that seemed to be a positive trigger for him.

CEO: OK, if it's not fear, what is it?

Coach: It's trapped energy. It's like, before you get up in a front of a big group, you put a plastic spaceman's bubble over your head. Your ego has to protect itself, as your friend Marc Andreessen recently said to another group I was with. You don't want to mess up.

How does it feel to breathe with a plastic bubble around your head? Shortness of breath? (*Yes.*) Feel a little foggy? (*Yeah.*) And when you talk, how does it sound? (*A little tinny, like it's not quite my voice.*)

However, when you get going and get comfortable, or when you're speaking to a group you know well, you take the bubble off, and you feel fine. (*Nodding yeah.*)

So, what you used to think of as nervousness—a form of fear—you now understand is just trapped energy. It's *your* filter and shield wrapped entirely around yourself, to protect *you*. The solution to being trapped in your own energy is to lower your guard (your filter), take off the spaceman's bubble, and focus on the audience. You don't matter when you are the speaker.

Like a lot of people, you know your stuff well, but you stay in your own head. Instead, focus on *how to get the content from your head into their heads*. Trying new ideas and mastering techniques that work for you will give you confidence, both consciously and subconsciously, so that you never need to put the bubble on again.

Oh, you will still have creative tension. A big moment, a big speech, a big interview—you will always have some energy around what you want to do. But it will be a more fun, creative tension—not the kind of tension that is *not fun*.

We know that this technique of *getting over yourself* works because our coaches have heard countless success stories. I'll share this one from someone I coach who is one of the top business investors in the world.

> Bill, you would have been proud of me and laughed at the same time. I was in the back of a room, about to talk to a couple of hundred students at Wharton. I know what you said, *they* should be nervous to hear *me*, not the other way around, but that feeling of fear—sorry, trapped energy—started to kick in all over again as they were getting ready to introduce me. Then I just said my three words to myself out loud—there was one other guy in the back of the room who must have thought I was crazy. And it worked. The three words for me were, "I don't matter." And instead of the energy bouncing back, I became focused on the students, what I was going to say that could be of help to them. And I pictured them as alligators. Now it works all the time.

(*Alligators?!* We will get to that later.)

I have heard of other techniques for overcoming nervousness. One is to take a deep breath, the theory being that the extra oxygen will calm your brain. This works well if you are focused on the audience and how you want to deliver your message, but not so well, for obvious reasons, if you have the bubble on. Another technique we have all heard is to imagine the audience members in their underwear. I don't personally recommend doing this. But if it works, why does it work?

It works because there is a ranking of emotions. Imagine a cloud in your mind, the cloud being whatever emotion you are feeling. Your brain can't hold more than one emotion, one cloud. Some emotions are stronger than others, and if a stronger cloud blows in, it pushes away the weaker ones.

There are some emotions that are stronger than fear. Can you guess what they are? Write a guess or two: _____

_____

Think of the strongest emotions you feel:

Love

Anger

Laughter

Have you ever tried to stop yourself from laughing when your brain thinks something is funny? It doesn't matter how inappropriate the situation may be, or how badly you want to stop laughing. It's just about impossible.

Now imagine that fear is the cloud in your mind. Love, anger, and laughter can be bigger and stronger clouds. If they all put up their fists for a fight, which one would win?

So the cure for nervousness is to think of something that makes you feel great love or passion. Or something that gets your blood boiling. Or something that makes you laugh (but for goodness' sake pick something better than the underwear). Those thoughts and images will drive out the fear.

Have you ever been at a school meeting when someone who appears to be too shy to ever speak up and say anything at all suddenly speaks up about an emotional issue? The person speaks eloquently, and afterwards wonders how he did it. It's because his love for the children—or his anger at something unfair—overpowered his nervousness.

In his wonderful book *The Trusted Advisor*, David Maister offers a slightly different version of the equation showing how our fear and our focus on ourselves undermine our connection with the audience. According to Maister, we come to trust experts based on the sum of three factors—how competent they are in their particular field; how credible they are (do they know what they are talking about?); and how much they care about us—divided by a fourth: how much they focus on themselves. You trust a contractor whom you might hire to work on your house if you think she has shown you that she knows what she is doing, can explain it well, and has your best interests in mind. However, even if all three positive factors are present, if the contractor gives you the feeling that it's all about her, all the time, then that trust is undermined. If the contractor has a sense of herself and an agenda, but in proper proportion to the competence, credibility, and care for you that she conveys, the trust you will have in her will be much stronger.

Apply the same concept to how we trust experts on any subject. If they know their stuff and can do the job, but they give us the feeling that they don't respect us, our feeling of trust is weaker. If they are brilliant, but every single story they tell is about themselves or comes back to them, our connection is also weakened.

What does all of this have to do with fear? Where you *focus* your energy is where your energy *goes*.

Focus on what you know, and on trying new things. Make sure the audience members know that you understand and care about them. Have a healthy sense of yourself and your agenda, but not so much that it undermines your competence and credibility, and the sense of caring that you want to convey to your audience.

Therefore, in worrying about whether we will do a good job or make a mistake, we make the biggest mistake of all, and the nervousness and fear that we feel about doing well become self-defeating. When you stop thinking that you are the focus of your presentation and shift your focus to the audience, not only will you overcome your nervousness, but you will be much more successful in connecting with your audience. The best method I have ever found for overcoming nervousness is also the core technique for effective public speaking: *focus on the audience*.

Not quite convinced? You are not alone. This is a difficult concept for many people because they have a few decades of mindset to reset. See if this story shared with one of the top casting executives at a major TV network helps. (One of the best things about this work is the amazing variety of people in cool places and industries with whom we get to work. Some of them we can name, but others we cannot for reasons of privacy. I have put a number of real-life group and individual coaching conversations in the book in boxes. They are all true, but the names have been changed to protect the awesome.)

Andrea: I guess I feel extra pressure because I hire people based on their ability to emote at a high level. I get flustered if I feel like I am being judged, maybe more than most.

Coach: (*laughs*) Well, on the question of whether you are being judged, now you know the answer.

Andrea: Yes, I am. So what? Who cares?

Coach: Exactly. And wanting people to see us in a positive way is completely normal and healthy. Here is one of my favorite examples. I don't know if this was your network, but do you remember a TV show from way back called *The Beverly Hillbillies*? My dad didn't watch much TV, but he liked that show, and I liked watching it with him.

Andrea: I remember it. It was funny. A good show.

Coach: In one episode, Jethro wants to be a double-O spy? He has a brilliant idea: to set up an office with a one-way mirror from his office to the waiting room. When he unveils it, he will be able to watch the people waiting to see him and the secretary, but they won't *know* that he is watching; that is his genius idea. In the scene that is so funny, he unveils the one-way mirror, but all they see is his nose and hands pressed against the glass looking around. Because he installed it . . .

Andrea: (*laughing with the coach*) Backward.

Coach: Yes . . . backward.

Coach: Andrea, that's you.

That is each of us when we focus on how people see *us*. We have the glass backward. Don't worry about how the *audience* sees *you*. What should you worry about? (Flip it around. . . .)

Andrea: How *you* look at *them*.

Coach: Bingo. Focus on you seeing *them*.

One of the things I love about public speaking is that there is no upper limit. We all have something to teach and something to learn. It is a microcosm of leadership and life. Sometimes it's when we truly focus on others that our magic really happens.

Don't be Jethro. To cure nervousness, flip the mirror around and focus on how the audience feels about itself.

C'mon, Bill, it's not that simple.

It's that simple. When you flip the glass around, take the bubble off, focus on reading your audience, and keep trying new things to connect with your audience, then your energy goes out to your audience instead of bouncing back at you.

Many participants that we have coached over the years have said that one of the most valuable pieces of the entire training is the concept of *getting over themselves*. But many of them also can't shake a preoccupation with the feeling that they are being judged by their audience.

One person brought up this topic in front of the class.

Kathy: I really like the concept of *get over yourself*. It takes the pressure off my shoulders, but sometimes when I speak, especially here at our firm, I feel like the audience is judging me.

Coach: You want to know the truth? They're judging you.

Group: (*laughter*)

continued

> **Coach:** You want to know the worse truth? Nobody really cares. Can anyone think of a comment you have heard at work in the last four weeks that was said so well or so poorly that it actually affected you? (*No hands go up.*) Nobody cares. It's not that they aren't nice people or don't wish the speaker well. Generally, audiences do wish the speaker well, but they are not starting *out* focused on the speaker. Who is the audience usually thinking about?
>
> **Paul:** Themselves.
>
> **Coach:** Exactly. What they have to do; the fight they had with this person; what they have to do later. Your job is to *get* them to focus on you.

Think of it another way. Let's say the purpose of your presentation is to hand out $100 bills to each member of your audience. The $100 bills represent your content. Would the audience members care if you gave them the bills upside down? (*No, it's still money!*) Would they care if you dropped the money all over the floor, then picked it up and handed it to them? (*Nope, it's still money.*) What if it got crumpled a little? (*Nope, they wouldn't care.*)

So what would they care about?

They would just care about getting their money. They want to get paid. To channel Cuba Gooding Jr. in the movie *Jerry Maguire*, what do they want you to do?

"SHOW ME THE MONEY!!"

It's the same with all presentations. The audience doesn't care about you. I don't mean that they are bad people and don't care about you as a person. I mean that they are just not focused on you in the way that you think they are, and the way that you, initially and naturally, start focusing on yourself. They don't care about how you deliver; they just care that you do, in fact, deliver. They are in receiving mode, rather selfish and passive in a sense, caring only about what they receive, what they get from your presentation. The function of good technique is to make sure that your delivery mode *delivers* the content to the audience. Grab their attention.

Sometimes I hear, "But, Bill, you don't know me. I don't *like* being the center of attention."

I don't care what you like. It's not about you. When you speak, it doesn't matter if it's six people in a meeting, six hundred at a conference, or six million on television; your *job* is to command attention. Stop thinking that it's about you, and that is when your greatness will emerge.

And if you don't feel comfortable commanding attention, I have a simple solution.

Don't speak.

But if you have something worth saying, it's your job to command the room. Do your job, my friend. Do your job.

Have you ever sat in a boring meeting? Have you ever heard a boring lecture or sermon? Do we need more boring in the world? Then, when *you* talk, own the room. Don't rent the room, baby! Own it.

Right before you speak, imagine that you are on a stage and that there is someone in the rafters shining a spotlight. You snap your fingers and command him to point the spotlight at you, then point it wherever your words, face, and hands point. You want to pull the spotlight onto yourself. Once you have the spotlight, you can do so much with it. You can redirect the spotlight onto the audience, to a slide, onto a specific person, into a story, back onto yourself, and back to the audience.

There are a million things you can do with the spotlight to get your message across, but you can't do anything with it unless you have it.

And you can't have it unless you command it. My friend Shakim Compere, CEO of Flavor Unit Records, which he founded with Queen Latifah (the wonderful Dana Owens), says, "You don't get what you deserve in business; you get what you negotiate."

In speaking, similarly, you *get* the attention of the audience when you *command* it and enjoy doing it. It's a rush for you, but it's for the audience's benefit.

So the secret is for you to *stop caring* too. Care about what you say and to whom you are saying it, but stop caring about how your audience perceives you.

These issues are not limited to our feelings about speaking in front of groups. I often see people struggling with what they perceive to be difficult situations—a conflict with a colleague or a boss, or even a set of opportunities—that they do not want to confront. Usually, the problem is with a person, a boss. There is a conflict, but the person feels he can't talk to his boss. It's easier to let it go, to not try to fix it. But, the conflict does not go away. Instead, it tortures the person, gnawing at him.

This is what was happening to "Steve," a participant in one of our classes who had to suffer through another long-winded Bill story to get some help.

Steve: I just can't work with Ned. He really, really bothers me. I've tried. Oh, how I've tried, but he took credit for the project we all worked on even though he hardly did anything. He . . . (Steve recounts what a horrible person Ned is and all the evil things Ned has done.)

Coach: Can I tell you a story and ask you a question?

Steve: (*laughing*) Sure.

Coach: I remember as a kid watching a television show called Mutual of Omaha's *Wild Kingdom*. It was a nature show, and Marlin and Jim were two guys studying and helping Africa. In one episode I remember, they were trying to catch and relocate zebras. They set up a corral and tried different ways to herd the zebras in the corral, from land and air, but nothing worked. The zebras were always too smart and too stubborn and would veer away at the last minute. They couldn't catch them, even though it was for the zebras' own good.

Then Marlin and Jim got an idea to make the opening of the corral much larger, like a funnel. They ran a line of rope, about chest high, from one edge of the opening out about 300 feet or so. They did the same with the other side, so now the rope formed a large funnel opening. Then they draped paper over the ropes, making a paper wall.

Then they got back in their helicopter and started herding the zebras toward the corral. At the moment of truth, the herd of zebra was heading toward the corral and turning into the wall of paper. Now, the zebras could have run through the rope with ease, but they hesitated, turned slightly, and went into the corral. The guys jumped out and closed the corral. Got'em!

Why didn't the zebras just run through the rope? After all, the wall was only paper.

Steve: They didn't know it was paper. They probably didn't know what it was. I don't know how a zebra thinks—to them it could have seemed like something else.

Coach: Okay, but they could have trampled it so easily. Why didn't they?

Steve: They didn't *know* they could run through it.

Coach: Steve, what is *your* paper wall?

Steve: Walking into Ned's office and saying, "I want to talk."

Coach: I can guarantee you that won't make all of the problems go away, but it will usually make it better. If it helps, I can help you understand a little more about why the Neds of the world act the way they do. When you coach these people, you see things from the other side, the insecurities, etc.

Steve: I suppose, but . . .

Coach: Mother Theresa wrote this great poem called "Do It Anyway." My paraphrased version of her poem is, "People are jerks. Love them anyway." When you can recognize what they are doing and look past it to wish the other person well, it doesn't let them off the hook, but in a way, it releases you. It releases what they do from affecting you so much.

You don't have to do this kind of work for long to see patterns. Almost everyone has one or two things that block them from going to the next level, at work, and in life. But, those things are different for each person, and they are not easy things to talk about. We are buffeted by the winds of other people's behavior, but we can find our own calm. A coach provides a safe space for a person to think through those issues.

No coach has all of the answers, but a good coach asks good questions to help the client see the situation from a different angle.

Typically, after I use this story with a client, I will get an e-mail a few days later. The situation is not completely resolved, but it is improved. What the client believed the other person believed was not quite what the person was thinking at all. They are now on the road toward a better situation. In Steve's case, this new clarity will give him a little more confidence the next time he is confronted with an uncomfortable situation.

Okay, zebra. What's your paper wall? Go run through it and see what happens. Great speakers and terrible speakers both make mistakes, but there's one big difference. What do great speakers do when they realize that they've made a mistake? They don't care. They are not hemmed in by paper walls. It's not about them. Great speakers know that it's not what they *come in* with that matters; it's what the audience *goes out* with that matters. As expert political pollster Dr. Frank Luntz says, "It's not what you say, it's what they hear."

Communication is about leadership, and leadership is always about *courage*. Throw yourself into your content, your ideas, and your audience—and let your magic happen.

SUMMARY

★ Fear and nervousness put the focus of your presentation on you and act as a shield that blocks your message from reaching your audience.

★ *Get over yourself.* Let go of the idea that you matter and focus on the audience and the content. Lose yourself in what you are saying and the people you are saying it to.

★ Ask the people in the audience what they want.

CHAPTER 3

Lower the Filters

★

The success of your presentation will be judged not by the knowledge you send but by what the listener receives.
—LILLY WALTERS

T ry an experiment. Pick up a small object and hold it in front of you. Attempt to think *only* about that object for as long as you can. Allow no other thought to enter your brain except that object. It's a test of mental strength. As soon as any thought, even a tiny one, enters your brain, quietly raise your other hand. Ready? Go.

How long were you able to keep your thoughts focused solely on the object? (If you lasted more than a few seconds, you are ready for Zen Buddhism.)

What does that tell us about audiences and our brains?

Even when we are really *trying* to concentrate, our minds are excitable; they want to drift and move on to the next thing. Most of the time, audiences are not *trying* to concentrate on the speaker or the presentation; they are in a slightly more passive mode.

In the previous chapter, we discussed *filters*—barriers that both a speaker and an audience can raise that block the speaker's message from reaching the audience. Our brains use filters to block almost all of what is being said to us, and what we are hearing, at any given time.* When your thoughts moved away from the object, when your concentration gave out, that was your filter at work, coming up.

Today, your brain is bombarded with more information in one day than a person living during the Middle Ages had to contend with in a year—television, personal conversations, signs on the wall, texts, e-mails, background noise. In addition to all the external information coming at it, your brain is processing 10,000 to 12,000 internal thoughts every day.

It's too much.

The blob of cells between your ears is the greatest computer ever invented, but it still has its limits. It's not capable of processing all the data that are fed into it. Unlike other computers, however, the brain does not crash. In fact, it's incapable of shutting down. *Ever.* Our brains *never* shut down, even when we are sleeping. If you are a machine, and you are being overwhelmed externally and internally, and you cannot ever shut down, how can you protect yourself?

> The average attention span of an adult is 20 minutes.
> You can prolong your audience members' attention
> spans by periodically giving them a rest.
> This can be done by telling a story, giving a demo,
> or doing something else that gives the brain a break.

You use filters. This is where the human brain's other unique feature comes in. Unlike even the most powerful computer in the world, the brain is capable of determining what information it wants and needs, and what it doesn't.

Imagine your brain's filter as a plastic shield—semi-opaque, like a shower door, allowing some light to get through, but not enough to see

---

*In a study published in the November 19, 2009, issue of the journal *Nature*, the Kavli Institute for Systems Neuroscience and Centre for the Biology of Memory at the Norwegian University of Science and Technology (NTNU) reported its finding that the brain blocks and deletes distracting information in order to focus on a single thought or piece of information.

clearly. When we are in a meeting or in the audience for a presentation, this filter is up and down at different points, blocking some, most, or all of what the speaker is saying.

Your brain can't help itself. Even when we consciously like the speaker and are interested in the topic, its filters will keep popping up all on their own.

As you saw earlier, when you held an object and tried to think only of that object, your brain's filters were trying to come up. When you are speaking, you want the audience's filters to go down. When people's filters are up, most of your content is bouncing off the shield. When their filters are down, your content is getting through.

During any given meeting or presentation, the average person's filters *can be* as high as 90 percent. At that moment your audience is not hearing 90 percent of what you are saying. Of course, it *looks* as if everyone is listening. We are all trained from a young age to look as if we are listening, even when we are not. It's called school. And it's a skill that we have found very useful in our work, and in our life, ever since!

We've all been in meetings that drag on for an hour, where the people in the meeting are bored and distracted and filters were as high as 90 percent. When filters are at 90 percent, how much information is getting through?

Only 10 percent.

How long is an average meeting in your world? An hour?

60 Minutes x 10% Efficiency

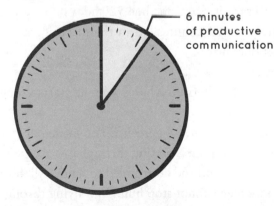

6 minutes of productive communication

Do you wonder why it feels like nothing ever gets done?

From what I have observed in the business world, filters, on average, hover at around 60 percent, but they can and do pop up to 90 percent or higher. However, they can also come down quite low when someone is speaking effectively.

An untrained presenter intuitively focuses on the area above the filter. That makes sense. That is the opening, the window of opportunity. The presenter then tries to ram information through the window, even as it is closing.

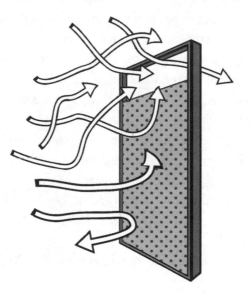

We have all seen it. Someone has 52 slides in his PowerPoint presentation. There are 10 minutes left in the meeting, and he is only at slide 23. What does he do?

He speeds up.

How high do the filters go when someone starts doing that? Give me a number.

How about 95 percent, 98 percent? The presenter is almost completely ineffective. Nothing is getting through.

That speaker is bound and determined to finish. All the king's horses and all the king's men cannot stop him from flying through the rest of those slides. The audience will remember little to nothing of this presentation. Its filters were up, and very little of the message got through.

I am not going to teach you how to ram information through the window above the filters. I am going to show you how to get the filters down. A very skilled presenter can keep filters in the 20 to 30 percent zone, but for easy math, let's use 50 percent. If your audience's filters are at 50 percent and you present for 20 minutes, how many minutes of productive communication will you have?

20 Minutes x 50% Efficiency

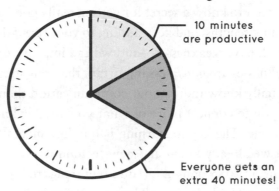

10 minutes
are productive

Everyone gets an
extra 40 minutes!

You will have 10 minutes of productive communication, which is *more* than you would have from the hour-long meeting in the previous example. When you lower your audience's filters, your efficiency skyrockets.

Unless you are speaking just to hear yourself talk, your job as a presenter is to educate, to inspire, and to deliver your content. It doesn't matter whether you are speaking to a small group or giving a speech before a large audience. It does not matter that *you* get what you're saying; it only matters that *they* get it.

Picture a bowl of fruit in the center of a table. The fruit represents the content of your presentation. Your job is to feed the audience. If you stand up and show the people in the audience the fruit, have you fed them? If you juggle some pieces expertly, have you fed them? No.

You have not done your job until your audience has taken a bite, tasted it, judged it, swallowed it, and digested it.

Now Back to You

At Own the Room we focus on our participants' *positives*, because we have learned through experience that this is the most effective way to improve. Most people focus, at first, on their own weaknesses. The first time most people see themselves on camera, they focus on what they don't like, what they perceive as their flaws. You are really tough on yourself, and that is okay. Being tough on yourself is a big part of how you have achieved so much. But you have to learn to balance that toughness with also being your own best cheerleader.

Do you want to know a secret for getting really good at this stuff? Focus on your strengths, and keep adding to your strengths.

Yes, we all have weaknesses—and we can improve upon them—but our weaknesses are *much* less important than our strengths.

You actually know more about communication than you think, and I want you to connect more of what you already know to what you are learning. The key to learning is building mental bridges between what we already know and new techniques. In the following exercise, write, in 20 seconds, a few different things that you think presenters do that are bad, that push filters up. Ready?

BEGIN.

_____

_____

There are many, many ways in which speakers push up filters. Here are a few that you may have written down yourself:

Speaking in a monotone

Reading PowerPoint slides

Using weak language and filler words

Not making eye contact

Having low energy

Now, take 45 seconds and try to write down four things presenters do that are good, that cause filters to come down.

_____

_____

_____

Here are some examples of effective techniques for lowering audience filters.

Make Eye Contact

If you are in the audience or sitting in a meeting and the speaker makes eye contact with you, it is virtually impossible for you to raise your filter. Your filter drops. Eye contact proves to the people in your audience that they matter. With eye contact, you are telling the audience members that it matters to you that they are there, that this communication is between *us*.

> Eye contact provides social information to the person to whom you are listening and talking. Too much eye contact and you may be perceived as aggressive; too little and you may be seen as having no interest in the person who is speaking.

When you are presenting before an audience, make eye contact with as many people as you can within the natural flow of your presentation. When you speak to a *large* group, make eye contact with people on the right, the left, the back, the front, and the middle of the room. Your whole audience will feel and respond to you moving your eyes around the room.

Eye contact doesn't just mean looking into a person's eyes. Imagine someone is sitting in front of you. Imagine looking into her eyes. Now, with one hand turned up, imagine you are pulling on a rope connecting the two of you. Use eye contact to pull the person closer to you.

Use Names

Have you ever been walking down the street or the hallway at work when someone calls out your name, but is actually speaking to someone else? What did your head do? It snapped around. We are conditioned to respond to our names. We have been well trained!

When you incorporate people's names into your talk, their filters drop and they are completely focused on you. It also increases your connection to the larger group, because the people in the audience are now on the alert that their names may be called. As you become more comfortable with this technique and smoother at using it, you can move on to a more advanced version: using the name of one person while looking into the eyes of another. You will drop both of their filters simultaneously, as well as the rest of the group's filters.

If you are speaking to 1,000 people, you can't learn 1,000 names. The trick in this situation is to learn a few names, and then use those names in your first sentence:

"Diane and Brett are going to visit a customer, Paul."

The filters of all 1,000 people will drop because their mirror neurons will tell them that those names are the real names of the people in the audience.

Care About the Audience

Most people believe that the speaker is the most important element of an effective presentation. After all, this is how we evaluate presentations. Was the speaker articulate? Could this guy tell a joke? Did she have charisma? The truth is that it is not the speaker, but the audience, that matters most. Understanding this fundamental principle will help you break through and connect with your audience.

Whether you're working with customers, employees, or colleagues, an effective way to lower people's filters is to make them feel that you care about them. Want to know a great trick for getting people to feel that you care?

Actually care.

This works amazingly well. They fall for it every time.

As you become even more of a speaking expert, you will start to notice the techniques that move filters. You will see a speaker tomorrow doing something effective and say to yourself, "I see what she did that made the filters come down." You will also become very attuned and sensitive to the bad habits that cause filters to rise. You will start to notice how many ums and other forms of weak language are used. They become like nails on a chalkboard to you. (Welcome to my world.)

*The sweetest sound in any language is
the sound of your own name.*
—DALE CARNEGIE

The motivational guru Dale Carnegie taught for years that any person will respond far more favorably to someone who has taken the time to remember her name and call her by name. If you want to be a success in life and increase your popularity, it is really essential that you master this ability.

There are many tips and techniques you can use to teach yourself how to remember names. You can find many of these approaches online. I know that some people find associating a face with a physical description to be effective in remembering a person's name, but I have never tried that myself. Here are a couple of suggestions that have helped me.

Most people can't remember names because they never actually learned them in the first place.

Think of a name as being a helium balloon. You are at a gathering, and first one person introduces himself, then someone else introduces herself, and then someone else. Each time a person introduces himself to you, it's like he's handing you a string attached to his balloon. When the next person hands you her balloon, what happens to the one or two strings you were already holding in your hand? You let go, and the balloons float away. The problem is not that you can't remember names, but that you never fully learned them in the first place.

To hold a name in your memory, use it in a sentence. Each time you do this, you're making another loop in the string until you finally tie a knot. Do this several times, quickly, and you will have a strong knot.

"Roberto, nice to meet you. Where are you from, Roberto? Roberto, have you met Dolly?"

Each time you use the name, you are strengthening its hold in your short-term memory. It doesn't mean that you will remember it for life. If it's important, it will work its way through the process by which you later solidify short-term memory, then turn it into medium-term and then long-term memory.

You can do this in your head, as well as out loud. Looking around the room, say to yourself, that is Dave, Dan, and Matt, then do it backward so that you are learning names and not just a sequence that will get messed up when people move: Matt, Dan, and Dave.

In meetings, people often introduce themselves quickly. A junior staffer will not interrupt to confirm a name, but what does someone with a senior mindset do?

"Sorry, I didn't get your name."

No one will be insulted by having to repeat his name. You have to be mentally strong enough to stop the train and ask him to say his name again.

See It Spelled Out

Because visualization is such a big part of how we think (half the brain does nothing more than process visual images), another effective technique for remembering a name is to see and spell the name correctly, especially if it's unusual. If you were lucky enough to be one of the first people to get to meet and work with Oprah Winfrey, you might have done a double take on her name. Opr—huh? Today, because we have all seen it so much, we can remember it easily. The same is true with brands, like Google, for example.

The same senior mindset that gives you the confidence to ask someone to repeat her name should give you the confidence to ask her to spell it. One of our coaches, Michael Balaoing, would say of his last name, "It sounds just like allowing, but with a B and spelled a bit differently."

The famous golfer Phil Mickelson is very popular among the galleries and the media, and not just for his skill on the golf course. If you watch him being interviewed, notice that he uses the name of the person interviewing him.

"I tell you, Tom, I struggled with my putter today."

Journalists are trained to make their work *not* be about them, but when a celebrity uses their names on national television, you can bet that it makes them feel special. Former Los Angeles Lakers basketball coach Pat Riley is another famous speaker who is known for using people's names when he addresses audiences.

It's a little thing, but that's communication. There are no big things in communication. It's all these little things that add up to big impact.

Large Groups

You are in the room with 20 clients. What do you do?

First, meet as many people as you can as they enter the room. Don't worry about hearing them all; just meet and greet them. Then, focus on learning the easy names first. This is what I do when I am conducting trainings with one of our regular clients, a large German engineering firm. I learn the easy names first. There are three women in the group, so their names are easy to learn. Then I focus on people who have a unique physical feature or some other quality that sets them apart or makes them stand out. Last, I learn the names of the six guys named Michael or Andreas.

Often, names are given in a round of introductions, similar to our "Around the Room" technique of asking each person in the room to take a turn saying something brief. Let's say there are 15 people sitting around a big conference table. As the introductions begin, turn your agenda over to the blank side and write down the names as fast as you can, making a rough diagram of where the person is seated at the table. During the meeting, silently memorize the names in short sequences.

Go over two or three names in a row, over and over, forward and backward, until you have them, then move on to the next group of two or three. Soon, you will have memorized them all.

When Giving Your Name, Enunciate

Have you ever had someone leave his phone number on your voice mail, but you have to replay it a few times to understand the actual number? As much as you want to remember other people's names, you definitely want them to remember yours, and they won't if they can't hear you clearly. You know now that the problem is not the speed with which you speak, but the lack of pauses. In enunciating your name, use micropauses. These are the key to enun-cia-tion. How long do the pauses need to be? Let's find out.

Get a pen. Pretending you don't already know it, say your phone number, out loud, at the same time you write it down, as if you were getting it off voice mail. For example, if I were giving you my office number, it would be . . . +1 . . . 973 . . . 975 . . . 4095.

Now you do it. Write it here in the book. Say the first three numbers. Write them as if you were listening on voice mail. Say the next numbers as soon as you are done writing those . . . next numbers. Write it:_____

How *long* it took you to write the numbers is how *long* you should pause between each one when you leave your phone number on someone else's voice mail.

Now do it with your e-mail address: _____
_____

Lastly, introduce yourself as if you were meeting a group of executives, using micropauses and enunciation: _____
_____

You should say your name at the same rate of speed that it would take for someone to write it down.

Who is good at this? Name a movie character who introduces himself very well, very clearly, with good micropauses, and with executive presence.

You could go with Forrest Gump, but I had someone else in mind. Here's a hint: his movies have had more sequels than any other movie (and no, it's not Rocky, or anyone from *Star Wars* or *Star Trek*).

Think British Secret Service: 007.

Exercise 1. Do your best James Bond impression and introduce yourself as . . . Bond . . . James . . . Bond.

Exercise 2. Now introduce yourself James Bond–style, but with your own name.

REMEMBERING NAMES IS MOSTLY EFFORT

The philanthropist and humanitarian Ray Chambers has the gift of an eidetic memory. This is sometimes, not entirely accurately, also referred to as a photographic memory, or total recall. If you have an eidetic memory, you have the ability to recall visual images with vivid detail and accuracy. If you are not lucky enough to have an eidetic memory, you just have to put in some extra effort. How do I know?

One of the people who travels extensively to bring Own the Room trainings to a global audience is Chris Hattersley. Chris, one of our tech people, runs all the cameras, dial-testing equipment, and other technical aspects of the sessions. Chris was amazed at first at how many names the lead coaches could remember quickly, even in the Middle East or Asia, where doing so is more challenging for an "American." He thought he could never memorize so many names. I tried to maintain the illusion that I was just so smart, but the truth is that with a little practice and effort, almost anyone can do it. He didn't believe me, but he practiced, and he became good at it very quickly. During one training, he learned 40 names by lunch—although, if I recall, there were a lot of young women in that training, so maybe he had a different motivation.

continued

Now Chris jokes that he could switch jobs and teach the whole training, since he now knows all the material and my corny jokes. When I ask if that means he thinks I could do as good a job as he does at running tech, his face gives me the answer. I am not smart enough for that.

SUMMARY

★ *Lower the filters.* The human brain blocks and filters much of the information coming at it; to communicate efficiently and effectively, you must lower your audience's filters and keep them low throughout your presentation.

★ *Connect first.* Before you can send your message, you must first establish a connection with your audience. Making eye contact, using names, and showing the people in your audience that you care about them are all techniques for lowering filters and establishing a connection.

Practice

Assemble a group of staffers, friends, or family members in a room. Choose a simple topic for a one-minute speech—your favorite childhood vacation, a story about your pet, anything. Ask each audience member to raise her hand if you make eye contact with her, and if the eye contact is really solid, locked in, that person gets up and moves. Keep talking until you get three people to move, each taking a turn.

You can also do this as a group exercise with your staff, taking turns delivering a short speech before the rest of the group. Then do the same with using names.

CHAPTER 4

Weak Language:
Cut It Down

It is better to be silent and be thought a fool,
than to speak out and remove all doubt.
—ABRAHAM LINCOLN

Here is the biggest tip in the whole book. If you learn this, and apply nothing else but this next chapter, you can improve your communication by 20 to 30 percent.

In English, the word is *um*.

In French, it's *euuuhh*.

In Japanese, it's *eto*.

Every language has some versions of *um*.

Why do we say *um*?

To think of something to say? As filler, to fill the space?

If you had to define the word *basically* to someone who wasn't a native English speaker, how would you do it?

Basically is a fancy way to say *um*. It means nothing.

Here is the first definition I want you to memorize. There are only two in the whole book. This is the long one, and it's one sentence.

Weak language is any word or phrase that adds no value.

So why do we use weak language?

We use it to stall, to avoid "dead air" while we think about what we are going to say next. We use it as a crutch, and we may have our own pet words or phrases that serve as our own crutches. And, we use it because we are uncomfortable with silence. Let's turn *that* completely on its ear.

There is a Spanish proverb: *the spoken word is silver, but silence is gold.* Silence is the *most* powerful tool you will ever have as a speaker. Little by little, as you become a more experienced speaker, you will begin to understand the power of silence.

So many great things happen during silence. The audience is digesting what you have just said. You are setting up what you are about to say next. The audience is feeling what you are feeling, subconsciously. Your audience gains all of its understanding of the words you've just said during the silence that *follows* the words, not during the words themselves.

For the majority of normal conversations and presentations, as much as half or more of what we say is weak language. It adds no value to our presentations and dilutes our message significantly.

The most powerful thing the average person can do to improve his communication is to identify and eliminate his own weak language. Seek and destroy. Have no mercy.

Examples of Weak Language

When teenagers use, like, weak language, what kind of, you know, words do they, like, use that can be a bit, like, annoying after a while?

Like, really?	Dude
That is *so* not true	I'm not going to lie to you
What-ever	So, anyways
To tell ya the truth	I go, like yeah, and she says . . .
My bad	Know what I mean?
Duh	Totally!
LOL, GTG, BRB, OK?	That is so not going to happen
Are you really going to go there?	

What does *any* of that *mean*? Nothing. And we all roll our eyes a bit when we hear them.

Oh, man, did we talk like that back in our day?

Then we grow up, go off to school, and learn a *much* better brand of weak language. Have you ever heard any of the following phrases at work? They sound very articulate and intelligent, but they actually mean nothing.

Let me make a point	What I'm trying to say is
Let me start by	In other words, let me just add
And this is just my opinion	At the end of the day, it is what it is
First things first, make no mistake	Like I said, I don't want to repeat
It takes all kinds, I must admit	myself
What I mean to say	When all is said and done
I'm going to tell you that	At any rate, that's the thing
Basically, my point is	Look, I could go on and on

Let's do a test. Pretend that I am standing in front of you and was just introduced, by name, as your trainer on public speaking. See if you can spot the weak language in the sample introduction that follows. Ready?

"Hi, everyone, my name is Bill. I am, um, really glad to be here today to talk about public speaking. Basically, what we're here today to do is to learn how to present well. I promise we're going to have a great session talking through the different techniques that can help you, uh, get better at your presentations. The goal is to improve your public speaking as it applies to the different ways that you communicate. So let's go ahead and get started!"

All right, did you spot the weak language? *Um*? Yes. *Basically* and *uh*? Yes, those too. What about the word *today*? Is that weak? It sounds like a perfectly fine word, but think about it. Was there anyone in the room who, before I started my introduction, did not know that today was . . . *today*? You didn't get the e-mail saying that today was going to be today?

Every single word and phrase in that introduction was weak. Even if the audience likes me and likes my topic, during an opening like that, I am pushing *up* filters. Why? Because I *didn't say anything*. I didn't say anything that you didn't already know. All audiences are prejudiced against the speaker. If the first 30 seconds of a presentation offers nothing new, what do we prejudge the rest of the presentation as going to be like? Weak language is not just a harmless habit. It's the number one obstacle separating most people from transformative change.

The bad news is that the opening I just offered is a standard opening in business presentations. We waste the first 20 or 30 seconds of our presentations driving filters up instead of down.

The average person has a vocabulary of about 50,000 to 75,000 words.

Let's Make It Personal

Raise your hand if you can think of someone in your life, at work or at home, who takes *t . . . h . . . i . . . s . . . l . . . o . . . n . . . g . . .* to say *this much*. As soon as she opens her mouth to speak, what does your brain do? The brain doesn't shut down. Ever. So your filter goes . . . *up*. Even if you like the person and what she has to say, you have been conditioned to tune her out.

Now raise your other hand if you can think of someone who fits the opposite description. He may not say as much, but when he does, he usually asks a thoughtful question, makes an important point, or offers thoughtful insight. At work or at home, when this person opens his mouth, your filter goes down. Write a couple of names that come to mind: _____

_____

Want to make someone's day? Tell him that you were doing an exercise where you had to name someone who fit the description of an amazing communicator and you named them.

Do you want the good news or the bad news? It's the same. Every time you open your mouth, at work or at home, everybody else's filter moves up or down, based on how much their subconscious brain feels you are using weak language. You have conditioned them. Even if they like you and like what you are saying, if you use a lot of weak language, their filters are going up. The single most important, dramatic, and rapid way to improve your communication is to identify and eliminate weak language.

In every training we have ever done, which includes sessions with our teams on five continents in the last month alone, we see every person make incremental progress at every single level. Everyone keeps improving. It's so much fun to be a part of it. But sometimes the progress isn't just incremental. Sometimes it's transformative. People take huge leaps. The person that everyone thought was shy steps out of her box and becomes confident and bold. She had always had it in her, but she learned to let it out. The person that everyone thought was verbose, that just could not shut up, and that everyone tuned out learns to be powerfully concise, and people start to hang on his words. As someone who used to be verbose and still can be at times, I so enjoy watching people master this.

The Taste of Weak Language

Let's try a little experiment. Fill a glass or cup one-fourth full with a beverage you like—coffee, soda, something flavorful. Now add plain water to the same glass until it is three-fourths full.

How appetizing does it look now?

In theory, it shouldn't be a problem. Water has no taste, so it should have no effect. The same should be true for all the *um*s, *basically*s, and other weak language. They don't mean anything, so what's the harm?

Take a sip of the watered-down drink. How did it taste?

That is what it tastes like to other people's brains when we use weak language. It dilutes and weakens the power of your message.

I conducted this exercise recently with a group of CEOs in Beijing. One of them drank the whole thing down and said, "Bill, I always put water in my Coca-Cola."

I said, *great!* One CEO in all of China waters down his soda, and I got him in my seminar. In Strasbourg, France, they refused to do it with the cola. I said, "C'mon, I'm an American. I *won't tell anyone* that you drank some soda."

They said, "No, Bill. We will not drink it."

I said, "What if I took your favorite wine from Alsace and then we poured in the water?"

"Then, we would have to *kill you*," one of them said.

We did it in Hollywood. We've worked with a number of celebrities, but this particular training was with agents. They turned it into a drinking game.

So let's play the drinking game now.

Let's start with a simple exercise, alone or with a partner, your call. I am going to ask you a question, and I want you to say the answer out loud, speaking for 30 to 45 seconds. Every time you use any word or phrase that you would consider weak language (*I think, well, um, I guess*), take a sip of your watered-down beverage. Your question is:

"What do you think you will be doing in five years?"

Ready, go.

During the in-person classes, the students often don't make it through the first 15 seconds or so before they are already sick of the watery cola. They will say, "Okay, you made your point. We use a lot of weak language. How do we get rid of it?"

We have tried everything with our audiences—all kinds of games and demonstrations to illustrate, and help them eliminate, weak language. The most effective approach, we have found, is to play the drinking game for five days. You take a favorite beverage and water it down to . . . *yuck.* You do this at work and at home. Every time you use any weak language, you take a sip. No one else knows what you are doing. After two or three days, you will see your weak language start to disappear.

EXERCISE

Take out your smartphone or tablet. Go to the camera and begin recording yourself talking for 30 seconds on the following question: What do you see yourself doing in five years? Then play it back and drink any time you hear weak language. Then delete the evidence.

Stick with it. Soon you will find yourself making a point in a meeting and then, as the meeting continues, think, "I could have said that better," or, "I could have said that in two sentences instead of five," or, "I repeated something." Take a sip. You realized it after the fact.

Eventually, you will find yourself *prerealizing* it and pausing more. Maybe, while you are speaking, you will hold up your hand to keep the floor and pause a second, so that what you want to say can click in your brain and come out of your mouth without weak language—more powerful and concise to your listeners. (By the way, holding up your hand is a great technique for signaling a pause to your audience. People will understand this, and their filters won't go up.) Now you are on your way.

Is it worth the pain of gulping down watered-down soda for a week to get rid of weak language for the rest of your life?

Only you can determine that. Our students tell us that the exercise is transformative. It's painful the first day or two, yes. Then, one day, the weak language was just gone.

Are you familiar with the poet Ezra Pound? He was a member of a famous group of American writers and poets who lived as expatriates in Paris during the first half of the twentieth century. Although Pound was famous for his own writing, he was known among his peers for something else. Other poets would bring their work to Ezra and ask him what he thought. He would take their poems and cross out any and all words and phrases that he thought were good, but not great, that didn't contribute enough to the power of the poem or the imagery or emotion that the poet was trying to convey. He would sometimes cut as much as two-thirds of a poem, whittling away until the poem was refined to its purest, and most potent, essence. Much as it partly pained them, the poets were grateful.

You need to become your own Ezra Pound and edit your words mercilessly. You do this already when you write. Editors play this role for writers. Like gold tested in fire, the final product is of higher purity. When you begin to notice your own weak language and edit yourself, you are on your way to eliminating weak language before you ever utter it. It takes some practice, but then you have the skill for life.

SUMMARY

★ Weak language is any word or phrase that does not add value to your message.

★ Eliminate the weak language that dilutes your message and raises your audience's filters.

★ Silence is the *most* powerful tool you will ever have as a speaker. During silence, your audience is digesting, processing, and understanding the words you have said, and feeling your emotions.

Practice

Assemble a group of staffers and have each prepare a one-minute talk on any subject of their choosing. Give each person a plastic cup half-filled with soda or juice and a bottle of water. Have them fill the rest of the cup with water. Go around the room and have each person stand and deliver her speech. As the person is talking, the audience members should indicate when they hear the person use weak language. Each time the person uses weak language, she must take a sip of the watered-down soda in the cup. (It is not necessary for the speaker to complete the full minute and be forced to drink the entire cup of watered-down soda. After two or maybe three sips, the speaker will have gotten the message and should be allowed to stop speaking. This exercise is meant to demonstrate a point, not to torture your team.)

CHAPTER 5

Strong Language: Build It Up

It's not how strongly you feel about your topic,
it's how strongly they *feel about your topic after* you *speak.*
—TIM SALLADAY

How fast can you read the text in this block?

Aocdcrnig to a rsereearch at Cmabrigde Uinervtisy, it dseno't mtaetr in waht oerdr the ltteres in a wrod are, the olny iproamtnt tihng is taht the frsit and lsat ltteer be in the rghit pclae. Tihs is bcuseae the huamn mnid deos not raed ervey lteter by istlef, but the wrod as a wlohe. Olny 57% of plepoe can do it.*

Interesting, huh?

---

*This block of scrambled text, and several different versions of it, circulated widely across the Internet in 2003. No such study was ever conducted at Cambridge University. The origin of the e-mail has never been determined, but, based on other research, the theory that it proposes remains a matter of debate. A researcher with Cambridge's Medical Research Council Cognition and Brain Sciences Unit maintains a website addressing the provenance and validity of the exercise, as well as additional research on the subject (http://www.mrc-cbu.cam.ac.uk/people/matt.davis/cmabridge); Keith Rayner, Sarah J. White, Rebecca L. Johnson, and Simon P. Liversedge, "Raeding Wrods With Jubmled Lettres: There Is a Cost," *Psychological Science* 17, no. 3 (2006): 192–193.

The human brain does not actually *think* in words or numbers. When we hear words and numbers, we convert them instantaneously into *pictures* and *emotions* so that we can process them, like a movie, in our heads. Then, when we want to speak, we process and convert our thinking back into words and numbers. It feels automatic, but it actually took us many months as infants to learn this one tool called . . . language.

This is obviously very complicated stuff, and there is still a lot we don't know about how our brains work, but for the sake of improving our communication skills, think of it this way. Words and numbers are abstract concepts that we, as a species, created a long time ago. As a society, we've added and refined words over the eons and are still adding words today. In 2013, the *Oxford Dictionary Online* added some new important words like *buzzworthy* and *selfie*. You know, practical stuff.

As the example given here proves, we don't always even *read* words; rather, we *see* them. Half the brain does nothing more than process visual images.

When we read, we are recognizing 99 percent of the words on the page from memory.

Here is another example to demonstrate that sometimes we also read in *sound*, not words. Read this next sentence one time—as slowly as you want—and count the number of times you see the letter "F" (upper- or lowercase, it doesn't matter).

> Finished files are the result of years of scientific study combined with the experience of many years.

How many Fs did you count? _____

The correct answer is six, but most of us don't see the "f" in the word "of" because we read the word as it sounds, *vvv* instead of *fff*. (If you saw all six, you're effing really good.)

What do these exercises tell us? They tell us that, despite our incredible facility with language, we *think* with pictures. When a speaker says the word *ocean*, for example, our brain sees a picture of an ocean—our own personal memory or vision of an ocean. When you *paint a picture* effectively with your words, it bypasses the brain filter and connects directly to the memory center of the brain.

Perhaps the speaker is using the word *ocean* to describe a happy childhood vacation, or the thrill of a big catch on a deep-sea fishing expedition, or the terror of being trapped beneath crashing waves. The speaker has now not only painted a picture in the minds of his audience, but also evoked an emotion. When you *evoke an emotion* effectively, you also bypass the brain filter and connect directly to your audience's memory centers.

When you paint a picture *and* evoke an emotion, the effect is twice as powerful. You earn double bonus points in the video game of being memorable. Bing. Bing.

Weak language is a bad habit. It dilutes our message and raises our audience's filters. We know this, and we now know how to get rid of it. It's like ridding our language of unhealthy fat. Now, let's put on some muscle.

The definition of strong language is the second and last definition I want you to memorize. It's even shorter than the definition of weak language, which we defined as any word or phrase that doesn't add value to our presentation.

Strong language is a four-word sequence—four words that we have already learned and discussed at length.

Say them out loud.

Paint pictures. Evoke emotions.

Imagine that you have a paintbrush in your hand and you are painting pictures with your words in the brains of the audience. Let's say you are describing the color of someone's shirt. How would we describe the shirt using weak language? We would say:

"He was wearing a red shirt."

Now, describe the shirt using strong language:

"His shirt was fire-engine red."

If weak language is one of the main culprits *undermining* our presentations, then strong language is one of the most powerful tools we have for *building them up*. Strong language is memorable; because strong language paints pictures and evokes emotions, people will re-member what we said.

Quick exercise: Film yourself with your smartphone or tablet look-ing at the shirt you are wearing right now and describing it in strong language. Then play it back and delete it. If you can remember what you said the next time you wear that shirt, you delivered the content with strong language.

Now, try to recall something that somebody said at work last week. Ask yourself, "Why am I able to remember this?" Did it paint a picture or evoke an emotion for you?

Setting a Scene

The first words out of your mouth in any presentation or meeting should be a scene. No warm-up or ramp-up. No, "Here is what we are going to talk about."

For example:

> It was late on a Friday night . . .

> It was my first day on the job . . .

> The client was screaming on the phone . . .

A scene can also be a question, a problem, a quote, or a statistic. What all these examples share is that they put the audience in the mid-dle of the scene immediately. Opening with a scene will evoke an emo-tional reaction in the people in your audience, and that is how you will lower their filters and make your connection. That's why it is crucial that you inspire them to feel the emotion that you want and need them to experience.

For example, let's say I was telling a story about my young daugh-ter to make a point about the differences between our generations in using technology.

My kids will probably grow up not knowing what an ency-
clopedia is. When my daughter heard me use the word *ency-
clopedia*, she said, "Encyclo-what?" I responded, "It's like
Wikipedia, but printed on paper." To which she said, "Why
would anyone want to do that?"

It's a cute story, but what did you learn about my daughter?
How old is she? What does she look like? Was she being earnest or
sarcastic?

Now imagine if I took the time to describe her:

Anna is an eight-year-old, dark-haired mop top who runs
around with abandon and has a smile that doesn't stop. She
doesn't hug me, she launches . . .

Whenever you introduce a character into a story, give a couple of
brief descriptive sentences, one depicting the person's unique physical
features, and the other describing his personality traits. Writers do this
in novels, so that the reader can form a mental image of the character.
You've done this successfully when the people in your audience can
form a picture of your character in their minds. Otherwise, they won't
remember the character.

Painting pictures and telling stories does not have to take a lot of
time. The more you practice it, the easier it gets. Ernest Hemingway
was once challenged to write a story in as few words as possible. His
famous answer: "For sale. Baby shoes. Never worn."

Remember, when we are speaking to an audience, we are not
bound by the rules of perfect grammar, and we don't need to speak in
complete sentences all the time. This freedom is actually one of the big
advantages that speaking has over writing.

During one training session, I asked a young executive to describe,
in front of the whole group, a favorite vacation from his youth using
only individual words—no phrases or sentences.

Matt: Shouldn't you strive to be grammatically correct?

Coach: That is one of the big *advantages* of speaking. Don't tell your ninth-grade English teacher, but no one cares as much about grammar when it comes to presentations. In fact, you don't even need sentences all the time.

Matt: What?

Coach: Come up here and I will show you.

When I say, "Go," I want you to tell the whole room about one of your favorite vacations when you were young. But you can't use any sentences.

Matt: No sentences?

Coach: Nope, just words; no sentences. And, of course, move around the room and use body language to help describe whatever you are saying. Take 30 seconds to prepare.

Audience, I want you to just count the number of words he uses— and see if he can do it without using a sentence. Everyone understand? Ready? Go.

Matt: Summer . . . hot . . . (*fanning himself*) . . . lake . . . girl . . .

Coach: Whoa, whoa, whoa! Slow down there, cowboy. Let me stop you right there. This is a family-rated training. (*laughter*) Okay, guys, how effective was he in setting the scene?

Melissa: Very.

Coach: How many words did it take?

Melissa: Hardly any.

Everyone laughed, but they also saw that none of the words he used to describe his memories of a long-ago summer were particularly fancy or complicated. In fact, they were pretty simple. The power of these words rested in their ability to transport us quickly into a scene, to evoke an image in our brains, and to inspire a feeling in our hearts.

You have two objectives as a speaker: to lower your audience's filters, and to orient your audience in the direction you want it to go. That's it. Everything you want to accomplish hinges on your success in achieving these two objectives.

Mirror Neurons

Scientists have known for years which parts of our brains we use to perform certain functions. When we do a certain activity, we use one part of the brain. When we do a different activity, we use a different part. A major breakthrough in this area of brain research was achieved at the University of Parma in Italy, when scientists discovered that specific brain functions could be linked to a single neuron.*

The scientists had wired a monkey's brain and found that whenever the monkey moved a peanut, a single neuron triggered the monitor. *Boop.*

Every time the monkey moved a peanut, that same neuron lit up. *Boop.* They were amazed that they could isolate as specific an area of the brain as a single neuron-synapse combination. Even more exciting was the accidental discovery that the scientists made when one of the professors reached across the table and moved a peanut. The monkey's neuron still fired. *Boop.* The team was dumbfounded. Why would the monkey respond the same way when someone else moved the peanut? It was as if the monkey couldn't distinguish between performing the action himself and seeing someone else performing the action. It was as if part of the monkey's brain believed that *it* was moving the peanut.

So, they looked more closely, and what they discovered, not only in all monkey brains, but in all mammal and all human brains, was something called *mirror neurons*. Understanding mirror neurons is such an

---

*G. di Pellegrino, L. Fadiga, L. Fogassi, V. Gallese, and G. Rizzolatti. "Understanding Motor Events: A Neurophysiological Study." *Experimental Brain Research* 91, no. 1 (1992): 176-180; and V. Gallese, L. Fadiga, L. Fogassi, and G. Rizzolatti. "Action Recognition in the Premotor Cortex." *Brain* 119, no. 2 (1996): 593-609.

important concept for becoming a great communicator that I want you to say that term out loud. I will then give you some examples.

Mirror neurons.

Explained in the short version, mirror neurons cause us to "mirror" the emotions we are observing around us on a subconscious level. This happens just about instantaneously. A very familiar example of mirror neurons firing away is what happens when one person yawns in a room full of people.

What do the rest of us do? We yawn. Why? Because our mirror neurons are firing. When we see someone yawn, our brain says, "*Me too.*" Yawns are contagious because of mirror neurons. Our brain says, "Hey, that's right. I'm not getting enough oxygen." (The other reason we yawn is to control brain temperature.) But it all happens on a subconscious level. If you fake a yawn, you won't trigger other people's mirror neurons to fire.

We all like to go to the movies or watch television. Do you ever watch a movie or television show and really *get into* what is happening, emotionally? This happens because a tiny part of your brain, the mirror neurons, thinks you are in the scene. Your brain knows that the action is happening on the screen, but a small part of the emotional part of your brain thinks that you are part of the action in the movie or show.

Are you a sports fan? Can you guess why sporting events are such a popular spectator activity?

You got it!

ESPN's tremendous success is due in part to the tiny parts of our brains that make us think we are in the game. (ESPN is also run by very cool people, by the way.)

I was once watching a World Cup match in a German town square where the game was being shown on a giant screen. There was a shot on goal and, in slow motion, the goalie was . . . reaching . . . over . . . to block the shot. I happened to look over at the crowd, and what do you think people were doing?

Exactly!

They were all leaning toward the ball, as if each one of them were the goalie.

I was laughing, thinking, "Guys, you are not *there*. You're not *going* to block the shot."

But, because of mirror neurons, what part of their brains thought that they could? (Just keep guessing "mirror neurons," whatever he asks.)

You are in a room with your family and friends, and everyone is laughing and having a great time. You make a joke, and more laughter erupts. At the same time, someone walks into the room. What does she do? She starts smiling, even though she has no idea what's going on, or what has gone on before she entered the room. Why? Mirror neurons. The emotions of the group are contagious, and they spread to the newcomer subconsciously.

Here is the final example I will offer of mirror neurons, and it's also a puzzle.

You're grumpy and irritable, in your worst possible mood. Suddenly, you find yourself alone in a room with a happy, giggling, four-month-old baby. The baby is smiling and saying, "Goo-goo, ga-ga."

What happens?

Most adults find that their mood lightens and changes quickly. Before long, they start to say, "Goo-goo, ga-ga."

Why does this happen?

Yes, mirror neurons; very good! But, why else? Why does the baby change our mood, and not the other way around?

An emotional battle between a baby and an adult is not a fair fight. The baby has all the advantages because babies do not have filters. They don't have words or numbers. They don't have any of the layers that we adults use to block ourselves from audiences. These filters function like panes of glass, separating us from each other.

All that babies possess is pure body language, sounds, pictures, and emotions, which are contagious whether we want them to be or not.

Okay, Bill, what does all of this have to do with good presenting?

Every emotion you want your audience to experience or understand has to come from *within* you.

Wherever you want to take an audience emotionally,
you have to go there first.

It doesn't matter if you're talking to someone one-on-one, on the phone or in a meeting, or to hundreds of people at a conference, or to millions on television. If you want the audience to go somewhere emotionally, you have to go there first.

Bill, I want my employees to feel a certain way.

It doesn't work like that. You can't put emotions into people. You can only draw them out. *I want my teenagers to feel more of a certain way.* Then *you* must feel it first, and some of that feeling will spread to them.

Do you want your kids to be fearless learners and livers of life? Then whom do they need to see do it first?

Whether it is confidence, anger, ambition, or any other emotion that you want to evoke in your audience, it has to come from *within* you. The people in your audience can "catch" these emotions from you because of mirror neurons. The emotion *you* are feeling will spread to them.

If you want to motivate an audience, who has to be motivated first?

If you want the audience to believe the data on the slide, who has to believe them first?

If you are confident in what you are saying, the audience will feel confident in what you are saying.

If you doubt yourself, it will doubt you.

But wait! I know what you're thinking. It's what Edward was thinking at a recent training:

Edward: Can the people in the audience affect you with their emotions?

Coach: What do you think?

Edward: I would say yes, sometimes.

Coach: Agree. If they are friendly toward you, you are inclined to feel friendly toward them.

　If they are hostile to you, you are inclined to feel hostile toward them. It flows both ways.

Your audience can absolutely affect your emotions. Everyone affects everyone else. Sometimes, as a speaker, you can catch your audience's emotions. The energy of mirror neurons is fluid. That's why *you* want to command the room and set the tone *first*.

Using strong language to paint pictures, tell stories, and set scenes are all extremely effective techniques for connecting with our audiences on a personal and emotional level, and keeping their filters down. After all, what is the goal of your presentation? Why are you up there in front of the audience? What do you want people to take away from the experience?

If your audience can remember what you said
three days later, you *educated*.
If your audience can't remember what you said
three days later, you just *presented*.

If you want people to remember your words, use your words to paint pictures and evoke emotions.

To quote the great poet Maya Angelou:

I've learned that people will forget what you have said,
people will forget what you did, but
people will never forget how you made them feel.

SUMMARY

★ Strong language paints pictures and evokes emotion in the minds and hearts of your audience.

★ Monkey see. Monkey do. We cannot impose emotions on people; we can only draw them out. If you want your audience to feel an emotion, you must feel it first.

★ Open with a scene. The first words out of your mouth should be a story, a question, a problem, a statistic, or a scene that pulls your audience into your presentation.

Practice

Gather a group of people—your next meeting, family dinner, or Sunday barbecue. Choose the person wearing the brightest article of clothing to be the "supermodel." Go around the room and have each person describe the clothing in one or two sentences. Ask the supermodel which description he or she found most memorable, and why.

CHAPTER 6

Demand Feedback and Love Video

You cannot teach people anything.
You can only help them discover it in themselves.
—GALILEO GALILEI

There is a lot we don't know about the brain, but some scientists theorize that when you sleep and dream, your brain rewinds and reviews the events of the day, running them through its supercomputer. It determines what to keep on file for later use and what it can delete.* Only the images and emotions that have really made a strong impression on us, even if this impression was subconscious, are saved. That's why, in our dreams, something that happened that day will occasionally appear in the same dream as something that happened 10 years ago.

For this reason, when we learn a new skill, we should immediately begin to practice it, therefore giving it a better chance of being stored in our brain. Scientists have not been able to find the actual engrams, or pathways, in the brain, where we store this kind of data, but they generally agree that this is how we learn.† When we practice a new

---

*http://www.whatisneuroplasticity.com/pathways.php.
†Michael Monteforte and Fred Wolf, "Dynamical Entropy Production in Spiking Neuron Networks in the Balanced State," *Physical Review Letters* 105 (December 31, 2010): 268104.

skill several times right after we learn it, we create a neural pathway that carves the skill permanently into our brain.

If you're nervous about trying a new technique for the first time— *what if it doesn't work very well?*—let me put your mind at ease. When you use a new technique for the first time, it won't work, very well, anyway. For example, if you don't usually move around the room when you speak, the first time you try it, how are you going to feel? A little awkward and uncomfortable. The people in your audience—via mirror neurons as well as body language—will pick up on your discomfort, causing them to mirror your feelings of awkwardness and discomfort. Your audience, then, won't feel that comfortable with what you're doing, either.

The only way to get to the mountain of smooth is to go through the valley of awkward. Don't go back, go forward. Persevere with the technique through a brief uncomfortable phase; you will quickly begin to feel more comfortable and natural. The brain is astoundingly adaptable. It's like knowing how to drive, but then learning how to drive a stick shift, a manual transmission. It takes a couple of lessons, some practice, some grinding and stalling, and then it . . . just . . . clicks . . . into your cognitive brain, and you can do it without thinking about it.

I guess I have some natural teacher in me. I can teach most people how to juggle three balls in 90 minutes. Or, if you can swim but can't dive, I can usually teach you to do so, fear-free, in 20 minutes. After trying out a new technique just three or four times, you will be amazed at how right it feels. You will feel comfortable, and your audience will, too. You will then own that technique for life. It just clicks, and you think, man, this is so easy, and you never turn back. No one who learns to ride a bike ever goes back to walking the bike.

One of the most difficult skills a human being ever has to learn is how to walk. In terms of the sheer number of body parts it involves, walking is quite complex. We cannot remember what it was like to do this ourselves, but we can try to imagine just how challenging it must be. Have you ever observed a baby learning to walk? He just keeps trying. He stumbles and he falls, but he never stops. Once a child begins the process of learning to walk, he does not stop working at it until he can do it, constantly processing the feedback he gets from his own body and from the environment, and adjusting to improve. There is so much work and effort involved in learning to walk, yet just about every one of us achieves it. The same is true of learning language. Learning to walk, learning to use language—both are inspiring metaphors for life. We can master almost anything if we stay with it, but we have to keep adjusting, based on the feedback we receive.

Imagine that you are trying to learn a second language. You practice and practice, but you have no idea whether you are pronouncing the words correctly. Without the right feedback, you have no way of learning the right way, fixing mistakes, or improving.

Golfers, did you get a hole in one the first time you played? Are you a musician? Was every note perfect the first time you picked up your instrument? How much do you think your family enjoyed listening to those early practice sessions around the house?

Practice alone is not enough. Doing something over and over again does not mean that we will automatically get better at doing it. Practice makes us more *comfortable* and polished at the level we are already at, but it doesn't help us grow to a new level. Think of all the meetings you have attended in your life. Did those meetings progressively improve because you held so many? Wouldn't that be nice. We can grow only if we incorporate specific techniques into our practicing.

In developing the Own the Room methodology, we have come across two enormously efficient and effective, simple approaches to practicing that will lead you toward rapid and exponential improvement: feedback and video.

Look at Feedback in a New Way

Bad leaders *block* feedback. We have all met people like this in our lives. They are not bad people, but they're bad leaders because they won't accept any criticism and they never change or grow.

Okay leaders *tolerate* feedback. They can't stop it, but they don't *really* want to hear it. They get defensive.

Good leaders *ask* for feedback. They listen to it, and they embrace it.

This is all true enough, but it is not enough. Not anymore. If you tell your staff, "Guys, I want to make my meetings and presentations better. If you have ideas on how to make them better, come see me. My door is always open," how many people do you think are actually going to walk through that door?

Not too many, if any at all. Very few people ever want to offer a critique to someone's face, even when they are asked for it directly—and this is especially true when it's the boss. It is easier for your staff to withhold feedback than to give it. We've all learned that it's better to keep our mouths shut, play it safe and be polite, rather than risk being *too* honest.

I was once involved in a project with the author, life coach, and motivational speaker Tony Robbins. I did not know him well, but we were in some meetings together, working with the philanthropist Ray Chambers, General Colin Powell, journalist Arianna Huffington, and Senator Harris Wofford—among many other wonderful people—for a project called the Presidents' Summit for America's Future, with all the living presidents, in Philadelphia. At the time, Tony commanded a $125,000 fee for a speaking engagement. I asked him, how did you get so good?

He answered me with a story about his early days as a young salesman. His boss required all his salespeople to give at least one speech a month so that they would improve their public speaking skills. Tony signed up to give three speeches a *day*, but he soon realized that giving more speeches was just helping him get more *comfortable* at the level where he was. He wasn't actually getting better at speaking. Few people ever develop this level of self-awareness, but Tony offers us a shortcut.

He then shared a secret of his success. He began to take a different approach to feedback. After each speech, Tony would grab a couple of people from the audience, take them aside, and ask them two questions: "What did you really like about the speech?" and "What didn't you like or what could be better?"

Often, Tony said, people would reply, "Oh, Tony, it was great. Don't change a thing!" But would that help him improve? No. He was prepared for that kind of response.

"I appreciate that, but I'm not fishing for compliments," he would say. "I'm not letting you leave until you each tell me one thing you really liked, that really stuck with you, and then one thing that just didn't work for you, or that could have been better."

Tony said that within 30 seconds, they would give him the feedback he was seeking, but first he had to push through the politeness to get it. He would then incorporate *that* feedback into his next speech. He built on the positives and addressed the areas that needed improvement. It was then that his career began to take off. Each presentation, little by little, started rising to a new level, and after dozens more speeches, always with this approach to feedback, he was at a completely new level, and always improving as well.

When it came to feedback, Tony didn't block it, tolerate it, ask for it, or welcome it. He *demanded* it. It was not an option not to give it. He pushed through the politeness to get it, and then it got easier each time.

Bad	Ignore
OK	Tolerate
Good	Welcome
GREAT	DEMAND

All right, let's make this personal. When it comes to feedback, where on the chart do you fall most of the time? It's hard to be objective about ourselves, but ask yourself, *hmmm*, how do I handle feedback in real life?

Do you block it, tolerate it, welcome it, or demand it? Write it:___

_____

Now, where on the chart do you *want* to be? Write it: _____

_____

Demanding feedback is the secret to success, not just in public speaking, but in many other areas of our professional and personal lives. You can't be good at everything, and frankly, who has the time? But, whatever you *do* want to be great at, demanding feedback can accelerate your progress. Do you want to be a better manager or parent? In anything where doing well matters to you, learn to ask those two questions: What am I doing well? What could be better?

When do you stop? That depends on how good you want to get at whatever you're trying to do. When you have reached the level that satisfies you, there you are. Consider, though, that the best athletes in the world pay out of their own pockets to hire coaches. Why? Why do they do this if they are already the best in the world?

Why does Tiger Woods pay two coaches to work with him, when he is already the world's top golfer?

In "The Making of a Corporate Athlete," Jim Loehr and Tony Schwartz discuss how professional athletes spend most of their time preparing and practicing, but a relatively small amount of time in the game, performing at a very high level. Most of us in the business world are "performing" all or most of the time, but we spend very little time preparing or practicing. To reach a world-class level, change that ratio.

Think about it. Think about how competitive your space is, and how much more competitive it is becoming. We are obviously focused on communication, but you can apply this technique to other leadership and life skills. What would it be worth to you to be significantly better at what you do for the rest of your life?

None of this is that hard. You can master all these skills now, or you can wait until later, but my advice to you is, don't wait until you are 82 and taking the classes at the senior center. The earlier in your career you master communication, the more you will benefit. Some of my favorite feedback from the companies we coach is that they didn't realize they could improve this aspect of their business so quickly.

One person from an international finance newspaper said, "Why didn't we do this 10 years ago? Not just presentations, all our meetings could have been shorter and our conference calls better. It's not that hard."

You have to throw the emotional switch in your mind to make it happen. You have to be irrationally committed to mastering it. The rest is just: *learn and practice, learn and practice.*

Feedback is the active ingredient in practicing; without it, we are spinning our wheels in neutral. We won't move forward or grow. Just like children's, our growth is not consistent or gradual, but comes in spurts. However, unlike children, whose physical growth spurts just happen when they happen, we must actively trigger the professional growth spurts that we want to have happen in our own skills, like public speaking and presentations.

Let's say you have been playing golf for years and you have a relatively consistent handicap. It goes up and down a little, but stays in the same range. The only way for you to become a better player is to take some lessons and have a coach break down your bad habits and help you build back up with better habits. The hardest part of improving is letting go of your old habits. This is tough! Your habits are habits for a reason. It takes force of will to let go and accept feedback, even from a golf pro.

Tony Robbins was successful because he not only was open to feedback, but demanded it. He did not let his own ego get in the way of his desire to improve. This goes to the core of leadership and success.

If you tell your staff that, at the end of the meeting, you are going to ask each person around the table to give you one idea on how to make your meetings more effective, everyone will offer an idea.

Why? Because you have made it mandatory, and they know it is now something that they have to do. You have made it easier for them to *give* you feedback than for them *not* to. They will think of something to say rather than have nothing to contribute when it is their turn.

In the business world, we can have so many meetings and pitches that it's impossible to have the time to schedule a debriefing session after each one. You don't have to. Just grab one or two people afterward and ask them two questions: "What did I do well?" and "What could I have done better?" But do this only if you want to get better.

Whatever they tell you is data for you to process and consider.

Tony Robbins *demanded* feedback. He would accept nothing else. This is the chasm between good—which is attainable without much effort for most people—and great, which requires a great deal of effort. Jump across that chasm. Here is your homework: demand feedback three times in real life, and chart your progress. By the third time, you will be amazed by the transformation you observe in your performance.

As many as 60 percent of people are turned down for a job because of poor or deficient communication skills.

Accepting Compliments

Are you good at receiving compliments, or are you terrible? Think of it this way. A compliment is not just about you. It's also about the person feeling good about giving the compliment.

My friend Jim Mustacchia, a brilliant executive trainer with whom I've had the privilege to partner, and from whom I have learned so much, has a great way of understanding this. Imagine a favorite aunt knits you a sweater by hand. She wraps it nicely and gives it to you for your birthday. When you open it up, it may be beautiful, or it may be hideous, but at that moment, what is the only thing you can say to her?

"Oh, Auntie, thank you so much. I really appreciate it."

What if you said instead, "Thanks anyway, but I don't want it."

You would never do that, because it would hurt her feelings terribly. You can decide later whether you want to wear it or hide it in the back of the closet, but at the moment of giving, you let her feel good about giving it. So you tell her it means a lot to you that she would knit you a sweater. You are not saying how much you are going to wear it. You are just letting *her feel good* about giving it.

Compliments work the same way. When someone gives you a compliment, "Hey, you did a great job on the project," and you deflect too much, "Oh, it wasn't me, it was everyone else," then what are you saying to that person about her compliment?

"That's okay. I don't want it."

What should you say?

"Hey, thanks, I appreciate it."

Use your own words, but say something that lets the person feel good. As with your auntie's sweater, it doesn't mean that you agree with what she said. It might or might not change your assessment of the project. You are just allowing her to give you the compliment, and you are receiving it well.

Finally, apply the same approach to feedback. When someone gives you feedback, good or bad, just acknowledge it. It's just a data point. There is no need to get defensive. It's a sign of mental strength to accept it. The mentally weak person can't do it.

"Hey, man, you might want to get a breath mint before we go to the meeting."

You could say, "Oh, you're saying I have bad breath? Me?! Well, I may have bad breath, but you are ugly. I can take a breath mint, but there is no medicine for ugly!"

You *could* say that.

Although, for world-class defensiveness and insult, the response just given would be the Winston Churchill approach, a take on his famous line:

"Winston, you are drunk and disgustingly drunk."

"Madam, I may be drunk, but you are ugly, and tomorrow I shall be sober, but you will still be ugly."

Now, in almost every other public speaking situation, you could do worse than to emulate Winston Churchill, but in this case . . .

You *could* say, "Oh geez, thanks, that's embarrassing. Thanks for the heads-up."

Feedback is a gift—of perspective. You don't have to *agree* with the feedback you receive. It doesn't mean that the people who are giving you feedback are *right*. You can process it later—whether it was helpful or not, a little or a lot, or not at all. It's just data. Sometimes it's very helpful, sometimes it's a little helpful, and sometimes it's not helpful at all.

Sometimes you will receive conflicting feedback. I call it the air conditioner feedback. Someone comes up and says, "The room is a little cold. May I adjust the AC?" Before he can even get to the thermostat, someone else comes up and asks, "Can we turn it down, since it's a bit warm?"

We try to demand feedback from our participants after all of our trainings, and we generally get very helpful insights from each session that help us with our own continuous improvement. Anything that was noted as good or smart in our training was probably the idea of one of our participants or staff members. Anything that makes no sense at all, I guarantee you, I probably thought of it all by myself.

But whether it's good or bad, at the time feedback is given, just say thanks, nod, and smile prettily.

Lights, Camera, Action

The second major source of transformative growth—and one of the most effective tools available to you for practicing and perfecting your techniques—is the video camera. At our training sessions, participants are in front of the camera constantly. We have had the honor of training many terrific leaders at innovative companies, but we are never the best coach in the room. That honor always goes to the camera. Just once I want to be better than the camera, but it hasn't happened yet.

We are in the video age. Just consider the video quality on your cell phone. You don't need a professional film crew to use the camera to your advantage. Your laptop and tablet should have video recording functions as well as your phone, and it takes only a few minutes to learn how to use them. If you take advantage of this technology, it can give you an amazing advantage.

Let's take it out and give it a try. Film yourself with any device you choose. Let's start with something simple.

Imagine you are giving a webinar to a global audience, representing your institution to leaders in your field. Give a two- or three-sentence introduction telling them who you are. Try to use some of the things you have learned. Use your hands to help you tell the story. Lean into the camera, and smile.

Record.

Now play it back—but you are *not* allowed to notice one thing that needs improving until you say three things you did well.

"Oh, okay. Let's see. I smiled. I used my hands to make gestures reinforcing my words. And I suppose, if I am being honest, I am *incredibly* good looking. There is no denying it."

Okay, gorgeous, now name one thing you could do better next time. Then delete the evidence.

Try this again, but stretch yourself this time—more confidence, exaggerated gestures, longer pauses.

Predictably, the introduction of the video camera at our training sessions causes a lot of initial anxiety and resistance. In every session, some participants will tell me how much they hate the way they look on camera and don't like watching themselves:

Ellen: Bill, I hate how I look on camera.

Coach: Ellen, you are terrific. You did a good job.

Ellen: I know, I mean, I guess. But I still hate watching myself.

Coach: I don't care what you hate; it's not about you. Oh, wait. In this case, it literally is about you, but still, trust me. It's normal the first few times you see yourself on camera, and then it starts to fade and you can start to see it differently.

Ellen: I doubt it; I see all the things I don't like.

continued

Coach: That is the other thing you have to do. Train yourself to see the positives in yourself and others first, before looking for possible improvements. With feedback, if you start with the suggested improvements and then cover what someone did well, that person will never remember the positives. We obsess about what we think are negatives. Both positives and improvements play a powerful role in getting better, but positives are far more important. Like my friends Wayne Meisel and Julia Scatliff taught me, "Three strokes of love for one stroke of challenge." Apply this to yourself when you watch. Physician, heal thyself!

It's perfectly normal, at first, to see only the things that you think you're doing wrong or do not like. Normal or not, though, it's not helpful. It's like rowing a boat. If you row with one oar and not the other, where does the boat go? In circles. What if you row with one oar, but faster? You go faster, but still in circles. Being tough on yourself is part of what has made you successful, but if that is all you do, you are going in circles.

So let's flip that around.

Pull out your smartphone or tablet and film yourself doing the following exercise. Imagine that you are being introduced on a video-conference call. A number of people on the call need to say hello and introduce themselves. It's your turn. Film yourself in only a few sentences introducing yourself however you like.

Now watch the video and train yourself to see the *positives*—*before* you begin to look for ways you can improve. In the in-person trainings, we are the *positive police*. Do *not* allow yourself to identify anything you don't like or want to improve until you first point out some positives.

Our obsession with the negatives—which is somewhat normal, and a defense mechanism—is also a recipe for failure, because whatever you focus on is what you head toward. *Where you focus your energy is where your energy goes.* Positives play a *much* more powerful role in your development.

As we get over ourselves, we can focus less on how we feel about watching ourselves on camera, and more on the little techniques that we do well and on the areas where we can do better.

You now have two tools that can change the rate of acceleration of your progress: demanding feedback and recording yourself. Use them and you will be giving yourself an amazing, course-changing gift.

SUMMARY

★ *Demand feedback.* After every speech or presentation, ask a few members of your audience: What three things did I do well? How can I improve?

★ *Use the camera.* There is no better coach than the video camera. Watch yourself on video. The camera shows you things that you can't see yourself.

Practice

Here is a simple exercise to get the ball—er, camera—rolling.

Think of a proud moment you have had at work. It doesn't have to be the proudest moment ever, but a moment when you felt proud of something you had done. Share that story in one minute or less. Film yourself telling the story. Tape it, watch it, spot some positives, and mark one improvement. Then delete the evidence.

PART II

MAKING YOU
THE STAR

With a solid foundation, we build the next level:

★ How to be a star and wow an audience with voice
   modulation and body language

★ Preanswering audience questions

★ The power of stories

★ Humor, your own personality and special sauce

CHAPTER 7

Voice Modulation: Find Your Inner Diva

*The right word may be effective, but no word was
ever as effective as a rightly timed pause.*

—MARK TWAIN

For this chapter, you will again need some method of recording yourself and playing it back. Your laptop or tablet probably has a video recorder. If you have a video camera, all the better. If nothing else is nearby, just use your smartphone.

Click on the camera.

Press the button to reverse the lens so that you see your beautiful smiling face.

Flip it from photo to video.

Okay, now do a couple of warm-up exercises. Read the following quote out loud and record yourself (for other quotes, go to http://www.owntheroom.com/training/quotes and select one you prefer to practice).

*See how nature—trees, flowers, grass—grows in silence;
see the stars, the moon, and the sun, how they move in silence.
We need silence to be able to touch souls.*

—MOTHER TERESA

Then play it back and notice three things that you did well and one thing that you could improve.

What do Whitney Houston, Celine Dion, and Mariah Carey have in common? Our coach Michael Balaoing points out that, as singers, they all have an incredible range.

As communicators, each of us also has a range, so let's understand what that range is and how to expand it.

Scientists have measured how much of our communication is conveyed to our audience verbally and nonverbally. Knowing that the number will add up to 100 percent, can you guess the percentage of our communication that is conveyed through our:

___ Words

___ Tone of voice (volume, speed, pitch, pause, and inflection)

___ Body language

Of our total communication, the part that the audience gets from our words is 7 percent. The *tone* of our voice—our volume, speed, and emphasis—accounts for 38 percent, and our body language—observable nonverbal gestures—accounts for a whopping 55 percent of our total communication.*

Of these nonverbal gestures that account for more than half of our communication, *half of those* are facial expressions.

Of course, as in all experiments, context matters. If someone came to your door with a giant check, balloons, and a camera crew to announce that you had won the lottery, his tone wouldn't matter so much. (The statistic itself is a bit flawed; the short version is, it has been debunked as inaccurate in other contexts, but it helps you see the importance of nonverbal communication.)

Put another way, 93 percent of our communication does not involve words. What does this tell us?

First of all, it does *not* tell us that words don't matter. Anyone who says that content doesn't matter is missing the point. It all starts with

---

*Mehrabian, A. (1972). *Nonverbal communication*. Aldine-Atherton, Chicago, Illinois. These oft-cited statistics will vary somewhat because every communication context is different.

content. Content is king. Words are important, but they are just the starting point.

According to the research, *how* we say something can at times be even more important than *what* we are saying. This should not really come as much of a surprise when we think about how we use tone to express ourselves, and to define and inform the meaning of our words, every day—when we are talking to our children or spouses, or when we are chatting with friends. Remember when Mom was mad and she would just give you the *look*?

Most of us do not go about our daily lives droning on in a monotone. We naturally and instinctively modulate our voices to convey excitement, anger, fear, wonder, sadness, joy—and just about every other emotion or experience. Many people, unfortunately, lose their natural instinct to adjust the tone of their voice when they get before an audience. Presentations and speeches are often delivered in droning monotones. Knowing how to modulate our voices throughout our presentations is one of the most useful and versatile tools in our public speaking tool kit.

Don't Use (Just) That Tone with Me

Tone is the volume of your voice and the speed of your words. Look at this board:

Determine where on the board you would place your own *natural normal voice*. Do you speak **LOUD** or *soft*? Do you talk really fast or very . . . s . l . o . w . l . y . . . ?

If you talk really **LOUD** but really . . . s . l . o . w . l . y . . . , then put your name in the top left corner. If you talk *really fast* but really *softly*, then put it in the lower right corner. Go ahead and write your name where you think it goes.

Now turn your video camera back on and record, play back, and delete a short story about a favorite holiday or vacation from your childhood.

After listening to your story, where do you think the *audience* would place your voice on the chart? Would it agree with you, or would it put your voice in a slightly different spot?

Invariably, the audience will say that the tone of your natural voice is a little different from what you think it is. The reason that others rate our voices in slightly different spots than we do is that they hear us the way we actually sound, and we hear ourselves filtered through the tympanic membrane of our own inner ear, bones, and skull.

Have you ever heard your voice on voice mail? Did you like it?

Do you think the way you sound to others is the way *you* think you sound or the way you sound on the voice mail?

The voice mail is how everyone else hears you.

Where is the best place on the chart for a great speaker or a newscaster to fall? Any guesses?

This is a trick question. It doesn't matter where your voice falls on the chart. There is no best place for a great speaker's tonal starting point. Your natural tonal starting point and your natural voice are perfect for you. Your perfect presentation is you being perfectly you. However, your voice should not stay in that one spot. If it stays at one tone—one tone meaning *monotone*—it is boring. When it comes to tone, a good speaker changes it up to complement, emphasize, and express the meaning of her words. Your tone needs to be in *harmony* with your words.

Word Groups

Here is one of my favorite quotes, by the social philosopher Eric Hoffer:

> In times of change, the learners inherit the earth, while the learned find themselves beautifully equipped to deal with a world that no longer exists.

Record the quote and play it back to see how you say the words. What did you notice?

You may have noticed that you naturally paused between certain words and phrases. This is because we do not speak in sentences. We speak in word groups. Word groups can be as small as one word or as large as several words, but in our minds, we naturally break down our sentences into smaller groups of words. We do this to convey meaning. To speak a quote, or any content, powerfully, it helps to understand word groups.

Here is one way Hoffer's quote could be broken down into word groups:

> (In times of change), (the learners) (inherit the earth), (while the learned) (find) (themselves) (beautifully equipped) (to deal with a world) (that) (no) (longer) (exists).

Now read the quote out loud, leaving pauses between the word groups. There is more than one right way to break down the quote, but word groups work most effectively when they are small.

Read it again, but make the pauses *even longer*.

Now try grouping the words differently, leaving pauses between the groups as you read the quote out loud. As you can see, changing the word groupings can alter the entire feeling of the quote, and can even alter the meaning.

Consider this example that one of our top coaches, Michael Balaoing, uses to demonstrate this point during his training sessions.

How does punctuation change the meaning of the following sentence?

A woman without her man is nothing.
A woman without, her man is nothing.
A woman: without her, man is nothing.

The grouping of words can have a profound impact on their meaning. It all depends on what you most want to emphasize. In writing, as in the previous example, punctuation is used to express the meaning of the words. In the example, the placement of the punctuation completely changes the meaning of the sentence. We use pauses to create word groups. The pause is a speaker's form of punctuation.

Volume

Earlier in this book, we quoted the poet Maya Angelou. Let's read that same quote out loud.

I've learned that people will forget what you have said,
people will forget what you did, but people
will never forget how you made them feel.

Now, let's break down the quote into word groups, boldface the words where we might want to speak a little louder, italicize the words that we may want to whisper. Where I put an extra set of parenthesis, I want you to pause for an extra half second.

Try reading the quote out loud again, modulating your volume and inserting pauses as instructed:

(I've learned that)( )(people will forget)( )( )(what you have said),( )( ) (people will forget)( )( )(what you did),( )( )(but people)( ) (will never forget)()()()()()(how you made them feel).

Notice any difference?

Loud Emphasis

Increasing our volume is one way to emphasize certain words. Using the Angelou quote, choose the words you want to emphasize and mark up the quote, indicating where you want to be louder. Use the following guide to indicate the range of your volume; read it starting from the bottom up:

100 percent: Screaming at the top of your lungs (boldface those words with three lines above them)

80 percent: Super-loud (boldface those words with two lines above them)

60 percent: Loud (boldface those words with one line above them)

40 percent: Normal speaking voice (do not mark)

20 percent: Whisper, clear but barely audible (italicize those words)

0 percent: No sound whatsoever

Now say the quote again, following your own volume chart.

You don't have to go from 0 to 100 to get the attention of an audience. It's not volume that drops filters; it's a *change* in volume that drops filters. Someone can be just as boring speaking in a monotone at 80 as he can be speaking at 40. When the ear hears a change, it perks up and tunes in.

Using Your Diaphragm

When we use our diaphragm to speak, we expel air as we say each word. We do this to convey passion and intensity.

Say, "I want to kick this ball."

Now, put one hand on your belly and hold the other hand forward in a fist. Start to say the sentence out loud. As you say the word *kick*, pull in your fist and say the word *kick* with enough intensity that you can feel your belly move under your other hand.

"I want to KICK this ball."

What happened? Did your belly move?

Do it again, not loud, but with intensity.

Now, count to five and see if you can expel air at the same time that you say each number. If you are doing this correctly, you should feel your belly move. That is your diaphragm contracting. Now count to six, but use the diaphragm only on the even numbers.

Using your diaphragm is another technique for modulating volume on a word.

The Whisper

This last dimension of volume is actually your *secret weapon*. When you use loudness or your diaphragm, you overpower filters with volume. That's why it works. But far and away the most effective way to modulate your volume is to *whisper*. When you *whisper*, the audience drops its filters to focus directly on you. It does all your work for you!

Whispering does *not* mean using a soft voice. It means aspirating your voice. A great example of a whisper is the voice Marlon Brando cultivated to portray the mafia patriarch Vito Corleone in *The Godfather*. Imagine that movie without Brando's brilliant use of the whisper.

When you are using a whisper for emphasis, try to channel your own inner Don Corleone.

Here is another key to whispering. Right before you are about to whisper, lean toward the audience, and pause as if you are telling people a secret. Then, aspirate that word group with a whisper.

Okay, now let's put it all together.

Here's our Maya Angelou quote, broken down into word groups, again:

> (I've learned that) (people will forget) (what you have said,)
> (people will forget what you did,) (but people) (will never
> forget) (how you made them feel.)

Mark up the quote using the following rubric:

Loud words = **boldface**

Diaphragm = rectangle around

Whisper = <u>underline</u>

When we teach this technique, most students can use loudness quite easily, but are uncomfortable with whispering. Once they overcome their resistance and try it, most of them find, to their great relief, that they can use the whisper to great effect:

Coach: That was good, but where was the whisper?

Richard: I can't do the whisper. It doesn't work for me.

Coach: Hey, Richard, do me a favor. First, try the vegetable and then make the face.

(Just to get me off his back, he whispered the last line of the quote he was doing to great effect—and great relief to him and applause from the group.)

Coach: Richard, nobody likes a show-off.

Speed

I want you to think of your favorite beverage, your favorite drink in the whole world. Now, imagine that you are parched, desperate for your thirst to be quenched. Someone walks over to you, holding a pitcher full of this beverage. She asks you to open your mouth, nice and wide, and lean your head way back.

"Trust me," she says.

How are you feeling? What's the problem? You said that this was your favorite beverage, and you're dying of thirst. Why are you so nervous?

If you had to choose how this beverage would be served to you, would you rather the person with the pitcher pour it down your throat all at once? A little at a time? Or, would you rather just pour it yourself? Why? What do you have, control issues?

When it comes to speed, all audiences have control issues. It's perfectly normal. When we read to ourselves, we control how fast we read to optimize our enjoyment or our retention of the content. During a presentation, the audience members need to regulate the speed with which they process your words to make your presentation a positive experience.

If that person with the pitcher attempted to pour the entire contents into your mouth without giving you time to swallow, your jaw would come up, sealing your mouth shut, and the liquid would spill all over the place. That is what happens to audiences when you don't regulate your speed properly or pause enough. The audience will close itself off. It will raise its filters, blocking part of your message.

To modulate the speed of your voice, let's incorporate three elements.

Superfast

The technique of saying a word or a group of words *superfast* can be very effective when it is used at the right time. If you're using superfast speaking properly, you never have to worry about speaking too fast.

As long as you enunciate, you can never speak faster than the brain can hear.

Staccato/Slow

Staccato means speaking one . . . word . . . at . . . a . . . time, taking a nice long pause after each word in a word group. This technique also can be used to great effect.

Pause

A pause is when we insert a ridiculously long moment of silence—in speaking, this is never more than a few seconds—between words.

Using These Techniques

Let's experiment with these speed techniques using our Maya Angelou quote. Read it aloud again, but this time, say the words that are underlined *superfast*. Say the words in bold slowly, *staccato*. Insert a pause where you see parentheses ( ).

> (I've learned that) (people will **forget**)() (what <u>you have</u> **said,**)
> ()(people will **forget**() what you **did,**)() (but <u>people</u>) (will **never**
> **forget**)() ()(<u>how you made them feel.</u>)

Notice that there is a pause between every shift in speed.

The pause is the most powerful tool you have in public speaking, because it has many different applications and can be used to achieve a myriad of effects. It allows you to shift between tones and speeds; it can help naturally fast talkers modulate their speed; and, when it is used to create a pregnant pause—an exaggerated moment of silence during which you pause before you complete your thought—a pause creates suspense and heightened interest in what you are about to say. It allows you to shift gears:

> **Coach:** Anyone know how to drive a stick shift, a manual transmission? (*hands go up*) Before you shift gears, what do you have to do?
>
> **Desmond:** Pop the clutch.
>
> **Coach:** What happens if you don't pop the clutch before you shift?
>
> **Stephen:** Krzzz . . . it grinds.
>
> **Coach:** That's what happens when you speak. The pause is your clutch. If you don't pause to shift tone, your presentation grinds.

Braking for Speed Demons

Raise your hand if you're a fast talker. Your whole life everybody has told you to do what?

You don't need to slow down. Your speed is your power. You just need longer . . . pauses. Technique-wise, there is a big difference between s . l . o . w . i . n . g down, which d . i . l . u . t . e . s your power . . . and *speeding/up, but/with* longer . . . pauses, which *increases/your* . . . power.

As we learned earlier, as long as you enunciate properly, you can never speak faster than the brain can hear. Speaking rapidly is not a problem. The problem is failing to pause properly in proportion.

Do you remember, from our chapters on language, the definition of strong language? The first two of the four key words are "paint pictures." You use your words to paint pictures in your audience's mind. But just for a minute, imagine that you are actually painting a picture. When you paint a picture for the audience, what do you have to give the paint time to do?

Dry. What happens if you start painting the next picture before the last one is dry? They will smear and run into each other.

After each thought that you share, after each picture that you paint and each emotion that you evoke, you need a pause. This is not for *you* to get *your* breath, but for the audience members to catch theirs.

In writing, a period is not placed at the end of the sentence to help the writer. It's there to help the reader understand that he's reached the end of a thought. It is a point where he can stop and digest what he's just read before starting the next thought, the next sentence. We don't have verbal punctuation. Pauses, and shifts with our hands, face, and body, are our punctuation.

For a speaker, the more powerful the thought that is being shared, the longer the pause needs to be. Otherwise, the audience members won't have enough time to process what you said, which undercuts the power of your message.

There are many other advantages to pauses. Over and over, we are learning the power and beauty of silence. A pause is not just about the audience members digesting what they've just heard; it's also about the speaker having the chance to set up the next thought. It creates anticipation. In physics, the phrase is "nature abhors a vacuum." Something has to be pulled in to fill the space. In communication, silence can pull something into its space. This works in your favor if you use pauses and silence judiciously. A pause held for an extra heartbeat *pulls in the audience.*

Don't be afraid to pause. You are worth waiting for.
Don't be afraid to pause when you ask the audience
a question. The answer is worth waiting for.

Many participants ask me how long they should pause under different circumstances. The answer is: your audience will tell you. You will know when a pause has been long enough from the audience's eyes. It is not the speaker who truly dictates the pace of a good presentation; it is the audience. A successful speaker will couple the skills of pausing and reading body language to keep a good pace.

Suppose you tell a joke, and the whole audience is laughing. You can't speak again until when? They stop laughing. What happens if you speak while they are still laughing? It's a double bad; they won't hear you, *and* you will undercut the power of their laughter.

Other emotions work the same way. When you evoke an emotion in your audience, you have to give that emotion time to breathe.

Laughter is the easiest emotion to read because our ears tell us when the emotion has finished breathing. The more powerful the emotion, the more time it takes to breathe. You have to read the audience's eyes. When people are looking at an angle (up or down), they are still processing. This doesn't mean you've lost them. Sometimes, this means the opposite. When they are looking back at you, they are ready for the next thing.

If you are a fast talker, you have to remember that when you pour a message, you have to give your audience a chance to swallow. When you evoke an emotion, let the emotion sink in.

The Pregnant Pause

A student named Jacob was concerned about pausing because at his company, he said, if he were to take a pause during a meeting, his co-workers would jump in and take the floor:

> **Jacob:** I understand about pausing, but in our meetings, he who hesitates gets cut *off*.
>
> **Coach:** Interesting. There are a couple of options in this case. You can hold up a hand to indicate that you are still speaking, literally holding the floor.
>
> **Jacob:** Hmm . . .
>
> **Coach:** The other option is a pronounced pregnant pause. Meaning, leave them hanging. "The client said the thing they are most upset about is . . . (*pause*)." If you pause after a sentence where it feels as if you might be done, and some people are looking for a place to jump in, they will. But they are less likely to do it during a pregnant pause.

With a pregnant pause, you create a cliffhanger. You pause in mid-thought and leave the audience hanging. If you pause in mid-thought, when you clearly have something else to say—something that your audience is now waiting to hear—others will be much less likely to jump in and steal the floor from you.

Voice modulation pushes many people outside of their comfort zone. Students will tell me that pausing, whispering, speeding up, and slowing down don't feel natural. The truth is actually the opposite:

Joe: These are good techniques for practicing, but they don't feel natural. They feel artificial.

Coach: Good observation, although it is actually the opposite. I'll prove it. Raise your hands if you have little kids at home—children, nieces, nephews, grandkids? Has anyone ever been little? When you read stories to little kids, how do they like you to read them?

Jeremy: With silly voices.

Kim: And body language.

Coach: Fast and slow, loud and whisper—and we can all do it. You are driving in your car, with no one around, and a favorite song comes on the radio. What do we do?

Anna: Sing!

Coach: And how do we sing?

Fadi: Loudly!

Laura: Badly!

Coach: Loud, soft, *falsetto*, bass—and we can all do it. But, then we get up in front of grown-ups and what happens?

Pat: We get self-conscious.

Coach: Why? Here is another secret. The secret to modulation is not just technique. It's permission. When we are reading a book to children, the children give us permission to be our full self, to use our full range. In fact, they demand it. "No, Daddy, read it again; you didn't do the voices." When we are alone in the car, or on the dance floor, or in

continued

certain situations with family and friends, we don't need permission to be our full self.

Adults, however, do not give us permission to be our full selves. We subtly pressure each other not to deviate from the norm. Here, the mirror neurons work against us. The world never gives you permission to be brilliant. My advice? Do it anyway. The audience likes it and we enjoy it, but we have to break through that little barrier of subconsciously wanting to obtain permission.

SUMMARY

★ The tone of our voices accounts for 38 percent of our total communication. Use volume, speed, and pauses to modulate your voice.

★ Pauses create anticipation, suspense, and dramatic tension. They give your audience members time to digest what they've heard, and they help fast talkers modulate their speed.

Practice

Read the words on the following chart aloud, using the voice modulation technique that the words indicate.

Voice Modulation Practice

Read each sentence below using the indicated modulation.
Experiment with pauses between word groups.

Bold=Loud   *Italics=Whisper*   <u>Underline=Superfast</u>   ALL CAPS=STACATTO/SLOW

1. We **don't** speak / in <u>sentences</u>. / We speak / IN WORD GROUPS.

2. WORD GROUPS ARE / a *small* number / of words / almost / <u>never more</u> / than five / and as FEW AS ONE.

3. Voice modulation / is when you make rapid changes / between **louder** and *softer*.

4. Staccato means / ONE WORD AT A TIME.

5. When you <u>speed up</u> / on some words / and SLOW DOWN on others / it *lowers* filters.

CHAPTER 8

Harmonize Your Body Language

★

True eloquence consists in saying all
that should be said, and only that.
—LA ROCHEFOUCAULD

When you are angry, slamming a fist on the table is effective body language, as is frowning or glaring, because it *reinforces* the emotion. Glancing at your watch while you are telling your date how happy you are to be spending time together is an example of your body language *not* getting your message across. And, a good way to find yourself in the doghouse.

Half of all body language is in the face. Remember the Motown singers from the 1960s? The lead singer is up front crooning the lyrics, and the backup singers, with their doo-wops and woo-woos, are harmonizing with the band.

As a speaker, your words are the lead singer. Your tone of voice is the backup singers, and your body language is the band. When all three are in synch, the song is magic.

Change Creates Energy

In the previous chapter on voice modulation, we experimented with changing our speed, volume, and word groupings, and we saw the impact that these variations have on our speech. Monotone—which means "one tone"—is boring. We have to vary our volume and speed.

Change creates energy. Just as the energy of a powerful summer storm results from a change in temperature, the energy of your presentations and meetings comes from your creating change: a change in position, in tone, in speed, in style, in tactics. The storm of energy that is *you* requires change to charge the audience. The more rapid the change, the more powerful the storm.

What would happen to a baseball pitcher, even one with a great fastball, if he threw with the same speed to the same spot, every time?

He would get smoked.

Any change you can make—taking off your jacket, modulating your voice, or just changing your position in the room—drops filters. It doesn't get your message across (you still have to do that) but it drops filters for a few seconds, allowing you to get your message through. This is because our brains are wired to become alert when we notice sudden changes, no matter how small.

You have already learned how to modulate your voice. Let's focus on other components of body language: using your space and using hand gestures.

Using the Room

When you move, you create energy. If you are sitting and then you stand up while you are speaking, the change generates energy. If you are standing and then you sit down while you are speaking, that too creates energy. If you start speaking as soon as you are introduced, while you are walking to the podium, that produces energy and immediately alerts the people in your audience to pay attention, because you are not going to be like most speakers they have heard before.

Stand up and ask yourself the following question.

Did you pay for the whole room today, or just that one spot? If you paid for the whole room, let's get your money's worth.

There are five steps I see most speakers use in front of an audience:

Standing in one spot. Most people start with the "mono-spot," the boring body language cousin of the monotone. There is nothing inherently wrong with this; it is where most people begin as speakers.

Pacing. The next step up is pacing, the "caged tiger" approach to public speaking. Pacing creates movement, but it is nervous movement, and it tends to distract the audience. When someone is pacing and talking, who is he thinking about? Where is his focus?

Exactly.

Such speakers are focused on themselves and their words. There's nothing wrong with that, but that is where the speaker's head is at, not on the audience.

It's better to step toward someone in the audience and then back again, then step toward someone else on the other side of the room and then back again. This will convey the message to the people in your audience that you are thinking about *them*, and that your presentation is about *them*. If you are in a meeting and sitting down, just leaning toward another person at the table will have an impact on that person's engagement in what you are saying. It boosts your signal.

Circling the audience. This can be an effective technique if the space allows it. As you walk around your audience, staying on the perimeter so that you are never turning your back on a section of the audience, the movement creates some advantages for you. Your body language is now commanding and forcing you to create new angles of eye contact with more people.

Moving with purpose. This is your ultimate goal: to use the whole room while moving with purpose. This can involve circling the room, stepping toward and away from audience members, or walking from either side of the room. The point is that you are making those movements for a *reason*.

For example, if you place a flipchart or a prop on each side of the room, you will have a reason to move back and forth across the room as you incorporate the different charts or props. If you are telling a story that involves a door (it can be a metaphorical door, as in opening up new opportunities or shutting out old technology), go to the door and gesture to it, pulling the door into the story.

Here's another example: Let's say you are telling a story about the time your boss sat down in front of you, looked you in the eye, and said three words that you'll never forget. As you retell that part of the story, pull up a chair, sit down, and *become* the boss. In each of these cases, there is a purpose to your movements. If it feels contrived, that's because it *is* contrived. But it works as you become more comfortable with it.

When you change your topic, change your position. You are a good writer. At the end of a sentence, you put a period. Why do you do that? Because your ninth-grade English teacher made you?

We use periods, commas, and exclamation points to indicate to a reader that a thought is complete, that it's time to pause, that we are moving on to a new thought in a second. A new paragraph or a new chapter signals a new scene.

You don't have these indicators when you speak. So you have to use pauses and shifts of your hands (and feet) to show the audience that you are now on a new subject. If you have three points that you intend to make as you are walking around the room, think of each point as an act in a play. Stand in a slightly different spot to make each point. Go linear from left to right as the audience sees you. *When we are giving presentations, our body language is our punctuation.* Synchronize your feet with your words, and use pauses and changes in your voice, hands, movements, and facial expressions to convey that you have moved on to a new idea.

Fill Up the Frame

In photography, the concept of "filling the frame" often distinguishes a competent photographer from an amateur. When a terrible photographer (like me) takes a picture of his child in a beautiful meadow, how does it come out? The child is minuscule in the photo. A great photographer knows to focus on the child so that her face fills the foreground. Faces on a magazine cover fill the entire cover.

In art, this concept is called "using the whole canvas." Most beginning art students confine their work to a small space in the middle of the page or canvas. As they advance in their technique, they learn to use and fill the entire space.

Likewise, as a speaker, you need to fill the "frame" of the room. You want to use the entire space.

Moving around and using the room is another concept that tends to generate resistance among some executives at first. (Do you sense a theme here?) One participant told me that he was not comfortable walking to the back of the room, behind the audience, because if he were in an audience, he would not like it if the speaker left the front of the room. I asked how many of the other executives in that course felt the same way, and a few hands went up, but not most. I told the executives that I was going to ask them the same question at the end of the day.

As we proceeded with the training, each person practiced moving around the room while giving a presentation. As they started walking while they talked, some of them even moved behind the audience. By the end of the day, everyone felt that moving behind the audience worked for him.

If you are not used to moving around, the first couple of times may feel unnatural. That is normal, but persevere. You do not want to be a mono-spot. Each time you stretch, you are literally expanding your range.

Hand Gestures

Appropriate body language, especially with your hands, helps you orchestrate a better tone. Lowering your hands when you are speaking softly or using your hands in a fist to give some extra oomph to a word or phrase can dramatically enhance the delivery of your message.

At trainings, people will often tell me that they use a lot of body language with their hands. We have all seen speakers who move their hands in repetitive motions, such as flapping or circles, while they are speaking. This is not body language. This is body noise. It creates energy, so it is getting you halfway there, but the energy is not directed toward strengthening your message. When your hands tell the same story as your words, your message comes into the brain in stereo.

Here is a simple exercise. Say the sentence: "I want you to think."

Now say it with your words and your hands at the same time. How do you say "I" with your hands? How do you say "you"? "Think"? Keep practicing until you can do it smoothly. You see how much more powerful the statement becomes when you synchronize your hands with your content.

Just as there can be many correct ways to say something with words, there are many correct ways to say something with body language. Many of us have a few excellent gestures that we use for everything. However you say an emphatic "*No way!*" with your hands is right for you, as long as it gets your message across. We can expand our range by adding more gestures to our repertoire.

As we have learned from these exercises, hand gestures are just one form of body language, but because people are more familiar and comfortable with using their hands when they speak, the subject generates many questions during training sessions:

Andrew: Is it bad to have your hands in your pockets?

Lisa: Yeah, what should you do with your hands?

Coach: Answering macro before micro, I have heard a lot of tips about hands. My recommendation is that you let your hands tell the same story as your words. Find your inner mime, your Marcel Marceau, your Mr. Bean, and have your hands, face, and body tell the same story as your words.

Lisa: So pockets are bad?

Coach: What do you think?

Andrew: Probably.

Robin: Unless your message is very casual, and you want people to relax.

Coach: Now you are getting it. You are becoming the coach, figuring things out nicely. There are a number of you, as we've seen in your videos, who tend to speak in stereo with your hands. Your hands are moving nicely, but one hand does the mirror image of the other. This is good, but change it up sometimes so that only one hand is making a gesture. Use more of the air space around you, but still harmonize with your message.

The best way to incorporate body language into your speaking is to allow your face, hands, and body to act out the story of your words. You don't have to act out every word with your hands. Just a few gestures that reinforce your words make your presentation powerful.

Usually, we want to be standing. Our voice projects better when we are standing, we appear more commanding, and we have a broader range of body language available to us. But there are times when sitting or slipping our hands into our pockets may be appropriate. Body language works when it tells the same story as our words.

To practice this, try speaking with body language alone, without using words.

The following quote is an Arabian proverb. Read it to yourself, then stand up and "say" the quote using only body language. Find your inner mime, your inner Marcel Marceau or Mr. Bean. Pretend that you are competing in a championship of the game charades. Act out the quote without words.

> Four things come not back—the spoken word, the sped arrow,
> the past life, and the neglected opportunity.

Now, divide the quote into "acts." As you "say" the quote with gestures and body language, move around the room, changing your location for each act.

Finally, layer the words back in. Moving around the room and using body language, also say the words out loud. Synchronize your movements and gestures with your words.

What do you find about your delivery?

Here is another quote with which you can practice this technique. This too is a proverb, from the Cree Indians.

> Only after the last tree has been cut down/
> Only after the last fish has been caught/
> Only after the last river has been poisoned/
> Only then will you realize that money cannot be eaten.

Stand up, and use your face, hands, and feet to act out the same message as your words.

What you do speaks so loud that I cannot hear what you say.
—RALPH WALDO EMERSON

What Body Language Are You Speaking?

Just as you wouldn't speak in Spanish to an English-speaking audience and wouldn't speak Greek if you were presenting in Japan, you want to make sure that you are speaking the body language your audience understands. Make sure you are using common, easily discernible, or easily interpretable gestures—ones that clearly, and unmistakably, convey the meaning that you want your audience to receive. You *do not* want to leave any room for misunderstanding or misinterpretation in your body language.

For example, pointing with one finger can be problematic. Some people don't mind it, while others don't like it at all. (The whole "gun" thing.)

We have learned that in any culture in the world, you can point with an open palm, face up, toward the person. This is a gesture of welcome and offer.

Our coach Manoue Poirier, who has an extensive background working across countries and cultures, advises pointing with your entire hand, fingers slightly bent and fused together, palm facing down. In this subtle gesture, you appear to tap the air in front of the person with your fused fingertips.

Even gestures that are common in our own culture can be questionable, depending on your audience.

> **Caroline:** I put my hand on a person's shoulder as I walked around the room. Is that okay?
>
> **Coach:** What do you guys think? Raise your hands if you wouldn't mind someone touching your shoulder like she did. (*two-thirds of the hands go up*) Now raise your hands if you probably wouldn't like that too much. (*the remaining one-third raises their hands*)
>
> **Caroline:** It would depend, then.
>
> **Coach:** Exactly. Know your audience. Some like it, some don't. For most, it depends on context.

The lesson from all of these examples? Know your audience.

Making It Yours

The first time or two that you try to walk around while you are speaking, you will feel awkward and uncomfortable. You can reach the mountain of smooth only by going through the valley of awkward. There is no shortcut for going through this learning period, no way to skip over it. The good news is that you can, and will, quickly master this technique. After just a few times, you will become more comfortable and feel more energized, and your movement will make the audience feel the same way.

The only way to truly own a technique is to practice it until it feels natural to you. Body language and movement can be practiced at any time, in any situation. The best people to practice on are the innocent people in your private life. When you order at a restaurant, greet your friends, or speak with your family, incorporate appropriate hand gestures and body language. To really own this, do it about 30 or 40 times over the next few days. You'll quickly integrate this technique into your repertoire.

As with all of the techniques we are learning, it doesn't take that long—a few tries—before you have it, but you have to be willing to practice. That's how we master cognitive skills. Try a technique and soak in the experience. Run to it, not from it. Go through it, not around it. If you power through the swamp, you will reach the other side clear. I promise.

SUMMARY

★ Body language accounts for 55 percent of our communication, and half of that body language is our facial expressions.

★ Move with purpose. Harmonize your movements with your message so that your body language reinforces your content.

★ Change creates energy. When you change something—your position in the room, your body language, or your voice modulation—you lower filters.

Practice

Select a quote or an excerpt from your speech or presentation. Practice "saying" the quote with body language—hand gestures and facial expressions. Now divide the quote into "acts" and move around the room, coordinating your movements so that you are in a different location for each act. Once you have perfected your body language and your movements around the room, layer the words back in. Synchronize your body language with your words. Film yourself, play it back, and delete it.

We have quotes you can use for practicing at owntheroom.com.

CHAPTER 9

Answer Questions They Haven't Asked, in Order

*If there is any one secret of success, it lies in the ability
to get the person's point of view and see things from
that person's angle as well as from your own.*
—HENRY FORD

In 1999, I cofounded an Internet company that was accidentally successful with two people who were much smarter than I, Michael Sanchez and Andrew Shue. It's now called CafeMom.com, and it gets more than a hundred million page views a month because of an amazing team. The company really took off when I stepped down, and I don't appreciate the obvious implications of that fact.

In some early meetings while founding the company, when we were pitching potential investors and corporate partners, we would go into meetings with our PowerPoint presentation, but before we started, we would ask the people we were pitching, "Do you want to walk through the deck or just talk off the cuff?"

Can you guess what percentage of the time people wanted to go through the PowerPoint presentation, and what percentage just wanted to talk, have a conversation?

It was about 60-40 in favor of the deck. Most people are wired to prefer a more structured approach.

How do I know what the audience will prefer?

Ask.

Oh, please, don't tell me I paid all this money for a book that tells me to ask the audience what it wants.

Yep. Every member of every audience is unique. Every time you give the audience members choices and let them make decisions, their investment in your presentation increases. Every time they put a little more money in the poker pot, they care more about it.

When I was going through the PowerPoint, I would say, "Feel free to kick me under the table whenever you want me to speed up or slow down, or if you want to skip something or dive deeper."

These techniques are part of a senior approach. A junior person focuses too much on her content, determined to get through it at all costs, no matter what. The audience wants to know about X, Y, and Z; the junior person plans to get to that, but first she wants to talk about A, B, and C. What is the problem with this approach? The problem is that the audience members' questions about X, Y, and Z may block them from hearing the things you want them to hear about A, B, and C. A senior person focuses first on the audience (or at least references them and sets them up), and then chooses an approach from a range of good options.

For your next presentation, ask yourself what decisions you can let the audience make. Here are a couple of simple ones:

> **Decisions regarding time.** *"Folks, we have 20 minutes set aside for a break. Do you want a couple of 10-minute breaks or one longer one?"*
>
> Don't drag this out into a discussion, but determine it by a quick vote, if there is not an obvious consensus within the first few seconds.
>
> I will also, just to change it up, pick on a person.
>
> "Okay, guys, we are going to take a short break. How long the break will be, will be determined by Judy and only Judy. So, if you have an opinion on how long it should be, send Judy a telepathic message. Okay, Judy. How long is the break?"

Decisions regarding order. *"We have the following three topics to go through. It doesn't matter to me, so does anyone have a strong preference on which to start with?"*

This decision engages everyone quickly because they have to think about all three topics to even form an opinion, which helps you get them interested in the topics.

Decisions regarding logistics. *"We need to order food. Any preferences? Who wants to handle this? Roberto? Great! If you have input, share it with Roberto during the break and let's get back to the agenda."*

Put Yourself in *Their* . . . Chairs

There is a concept in psychology known as high and low self-monitoring. We are being high self-monitors when we are attuning ourselves to what others are thinking of us. We are low self-monitors when we are oblivious to it.

In your continuous efforts to keep your focus on the audience, and to remind yourself that your presentation is about the audience, consider what you would think if you were physically in your own audience. Walk over to a chair where your audience was or would be seated, and look up at where you were standing during your presentation. The more you see yourself as the people in your audience see you, and ask yourself what they might be thinking, the more breakthroughs and improvements you will discover in your presentation and speaking skills.

Keep asking yourself, "If I were in the audience, what would I be thinking?"

This is not the same as worrying about what the audience thinks of *you*, or how it is judging you. Now that we know we are being judged, we just don't care.

Audiences often have questions that they just won't ask the speaker for a variety of reasons. When you figure out what those questions are and answer them without being asked, you look smart. *Answer the questions the audience members do not ask, in the order in which they are not asking them.*

Wait, what does that mean?

If you are pitching or selling something, people may wonder:

> "Why does your product cost what it does?"

> "How are you better than your competitors?"

> "What do you get out of this sale?"

Your audience members are not going to ask these questions out loud, but they will be thinking about them, and this will block out some of what you are saying to them.

Almost all audiences are asking some form of just three simple questions:

> What? (What is this about?)

> So what? (How is this relevant to me?)

> What's next? (What do I do with this?)

You can use your audience members' unanswered questions to your advantage as you see their filters going up.

Let's say you are presenting, and you were supposed to stop at noon for a one-hour lunch. It's 12:10, and you're still yapping. What question would your audience *not* be asking?

> ("Uh, *when* are we stopping for lunch?")

> ("Man, when is this person going to *stop*?!")

These are completely natural questions for an audience to have. Politeness prevents folks from asking you these questions, but their filters are high because those unasked and unanswered questions are blocking them from really hearing you.

If you recognize this, you can turn it around to your advantage. You can say, "Guys, I know we are ten minutes over. If you can give me five more minutes, we can finish this whole section and still take one solid hour for lunch. Is that okay with everyone?"

If you do that, in what direction would the audience's filters move? They'd go down.

When you are interested in an object, your pupils will dilate.
This is a big cue for salespeople all over the world.

We may laugh at the classic stereotype of a car salesman, but we can learn from the techniques. You go to a car dealership and stand next to a red convertible. The schmaltzy car salesman ambles over, tugs on his belt, and asks . . .

"What do I have to do to put *you* behind the wheel of this shiny new car?"

It's a brilliant question. Why?

Because your answer tells him your main buying criterion. If you say, "Well, it had better get good gas mileage," what does he now know is your number one criterion? If you say, "Oh, I can't afford it," what does he now understand is your top criterion? Price point.

There is a difference between being smart and being wise. Instead of showing people how smart you are by *guessing* at what they care about, show them how *wise* you are by *asking them* and listening.

Let's say you are doing a PowerPoint and someone raises a question that you know you are going to address five slides later. How do most of us respond?

"I will come to that later."

Which is a polite way of saying, what?

"Shut up. This is *my* PowerPoint. I worked on it all weekend, so kindly don't interrupt again."

Sometimes we even try to use the Jedi mind trick.

We say, "Yes, we will come to that later," or, "Ask that question again when we come to that slide."

They nod, as if to say, "Great! That was my plan all along."

"These are not the droids you are looking for."

There are, of course, times when the order of our slides does matter, or when it is important to adhere to the specific format we've designed for our presentation, but in most cases, it matters less than we think it does, and *much less* than the chance to increase our engagement with our audience. In those times, you could respond to an "out of order" question by saying, "Great question; shall we jump there?" Then jump to the slide that applies to the matter and address the issue. You also want to stop and consider the fact that the question came up earlier in the presentation than you thought it would. That's an important tidbit of feedback. You may want to move that slide up the next time you give that presentation, if you see a pattern.

You shouldn't dread or be thrown off by interruptions or questions. In fact, you *want* to let the audience interrupt, and for a very good reason. Every time you allow the members of your audience to make a decision, you strengthen your connection with them. Think of it like a poker game. If the audience members get to put some money in the pot, then they become invested. Conversely, every time you *block* the audience members from making a decision, you weaken your connection with them.

It's like a cell phone signal. If you have four or five bars, you have a great conversation. If you have between one and two bars (the average presentation), the connection is spotty. Imagine that every time the audience members get to make a decision, the signal strengthens a bar or two. When you block them from making a decision, it drops a bar.

HOSTILE QUESTIONS

We all get hit sometimes with questions that are hostile, confusing, or challenging—or for which we're simply just not prepared. This can happen in a meeting or an interview, on a panel, or even during a keynote. Don't worry. With a couple of easy tips, we can help you sail through these rough seas.

The key is to keep your balance and buy yourself a few seconds to think. There are a couple of simple techniques to help you buy this time. These same techniques can also be used if you ever lose your place in a presentation.

Deflect to someone else.

Let's say you get asked, "What do you think we should do about X?"

You are not sure what you think, and you don't have an answer on the tip of your tongue. To buy time, deflect the question to either the whole group, a subset of the group, or a specific person.

What do you guys think? (Deflect to the whole group and get a couple of answers while you formulate your own.)

Ricardo (seated furthest away), *any thoughts on this one?*

Why pick someone who is seated far away? Because that redirects the focus of the group in that direction and away from you, making it easier for you to get your bearings and think of your answer. The person may not give a long answer, but often all you need is a few seconds.

REFLECT BACK

Once in a while, you get a statement disguised as a question.

For example, an interviewer asks, "Don't you think we are spending too much money on X?"

continued

You can see this is really a statement, disguised as a question. In good faith, and assuming good intentions, you can reflect it back.

Well, what do you think?

While the person is giving her opinion, you get a few seconds to formulate your answer. Allowing her to express her concerns also reduces her hostility a bit.

Feeding the Alligators

A good general rule in public speaking is never to compare people to animals. That's not nice, and it's certainly not politically correct. But let's do it anyway.

Smart people and strong leaders are like alligators.

Can you get alligators to line up and do what you want them to? No way. Alligators cannot be trained that way, and trying to control them just causes more problems. However, you can motivate them . . . if you know how.

Coach: How do you motivate an alligator?

Bernd: With food.

Coach: And what is their favorite food?

David: Humans. (*laughter*)

Stefan: A chicken.

Coach: I was going for meat . . . let's just say meat. All of you are like alligators and your meat is problems. I will prove it. Raise your hand if the following statement is true: in the real world, humility aside, you are kind of good at solving problems. If there is a problem, you can usually find a way to solve it when you want to.

Audience: (*raises its hands*)

Coach: Next statement: in the real world, you *like* the feeling you get when you figure it out, especially if you solve it before everyone else.

Audience: (*raises its hands and nods "yeah"*)

Coach: You are falling into my trap. Last question: in the real world, you are *so* good at solving problems, and you like the feeling *so much* when you solve one, that you are not happy unless you have what?

Audience: (*dawning on them*) Problems. Problems to solve.

Coach: This is a CEO's secret. When you give the people in your audience a meaty problem, they can't help themselves. They engage with you. By the way, what is the name of this actual town we are in? I came straight from the airport. This town is . . .

Audience: Feldafing.

Coach: Why did you say the name of the town? Because I dangled a little bit of meat in front of you, and you couldn't help yourself. Like alligators, you had to snap for it.

This also works in reverse. Let's say you worked for me, and I said, "I am the boss. Just do it *my* way. I don't need you to think; just do." What would happen? I would become the 1.76-meter piece of filet mignon. *I* would *become* the problem to be solved.

By the way, did you see how I used the metric system there?

Gonzalo: Yes, very impressive. For an *American*.

What's the point?

It's natural to want to show the audience how smart you are. It's normal! But when you let the people in the audience show you how smart *they* are, you've got them eating out of the palm of your hand.

This is a CEO's secret for effective leadership and public speaking. When you give the audience members a meaty problem to solve, they can't help themselves. They engage with you. Once they have the scent of a problem to solve, they begin to salivate over how good it will taste to fix it. They will not be able to raise their filters against the meat.

Unfortunately, this can work in reverse. If you have lost your audience members' interest, if you are not engaging them, or if you are acting as if you are the only one with all the answers, then you *become* the problem to *be solved*. One of the first ways that your audience may "solve" the *problem of you* will be to tune you out and stop listening.

The need to show how smart we are is natural and healthy, but let it go. Every once in a while, the boss is accidentally right. Let him be. The customer can actually have a decent idea. The people below you can improve on your strategies. Let them. That's what you pay them for. Allow the audience members to upgrade your agenda. Let them give you feedback on the spot. When you let others show you how smart *they* are, you get promoted from smart to "wise."

DISTRACTED AUDIENCES

At some point in your career as a speaker, you will encounter individuals in your audiences who are particularly distracted and perhaps even disruptive. Maybe you have two people who are carrying on a conversation. Maybe you have a guy who is obviously texting, or even talking, on his cell phone. This behavior not only is disturbing you, but is probably disturbing and distracting other members of your audience.

I learned this technique on six steps to engaging a distracted audience from my great friend Jim Mustacchia. Jim has done leadership training for some of the top companies in the world, and drew on that global experience, as well as his experience at Harvard Business School. There are two keys to making the steps work.

Assume good intentions. Don't fall into the trap of thinking that because someone is talking or texting, she is hostile toward you or not interested in what you are saying. I promise you that nobody wakes up in the morning thinking about how to ruin your meeting. The person has simply become distracted by something else, and your job is to attract her back into the fold. You will not be able to do this if you interpret the behavior as a rejection of you or of your presentation. Instead, you will convey hostility and frustration toward her.

Separate the action from the person. You want the talking or texting or other disruption to stop, but you do not want to reject the person who is doing the talking or texting. The behavior is unwelcome, but the person is very much welcome, and it's your job to extend that welcome. The more you separate the behavior from the person, the easier it is to change the behavior.

Six Steps for Handling Distracted Audiences

1. *First, just make eye contact with the problem child.*
    a. Send a message with your eyes saying, "We want you back; we like you." Be positive and warm.

2. *If that doesn't work, then go to DEFCON 2! Make eye contact and step toward the person.*
    a. This sends the same message—we want you back—but with a slightly higher level of intervention. If you are seated, lean toward the person.

3. *If that doesn't work, then move to stand beside the person or behind the person.*
    a. Not saying a word or touching her, but just being near her, while staying positive, has an effect. Stay presidential! Sometimes, it is not possible to do this in the room, but this elevates the interventions without you saying a word to the person.
    b. Most of the time, Steps 1, 2, and 3 will solve the problem.

4. *If that doesn't work, give her a job.*
    a. "Can you help me write on the board? Be the timekeeper?"
    b. "I'm going to ask Joe in a minute for his ideas on this; he has some great thinking on this topic."

continued

5. *If that doesn't work, you have a tough one. Use peer pressure from the whole group.*

   a. "Guys, we all agreed to turn off our cell phones, didn't we?"

   b. This is a very high level of intervention; you almost never want to go there. It changes the energy.

6. *Level 6 is: Take a break and talk one-on-one.*

   a. Take a bio break and talk to the person one-on-one: "Is everything okay?" Assume good intentions.

You may be thinking that this all seems like a lot of extra work, and that engaging your audience this way will take a lot of extra time, or that you don't want to waste time asking questions, telling stories, painting scenes, or tossing meat. You just want to get up there and get through the topic at hand as quickly as possible so that everyone can get back to work.

This was the concern of Andreas, an executive who approached me during a training session to express his concern that when he has limited time to get through a lot of content, socializing and involving the audience could waste much of that precious time:

Coach: Think of the last time you checked into a hotel on a business trip. You hustle up to your room and flip open your laptop to send an important e-mail. Can you just type the e-mail and hit send, or do you have to do something first?

Andreas: I have to connect to the Internet first.

Coach: Exactly. You have to log on to the Wi-Fi; you have to establish your connection. What would happen if you hit send on the e-mail before you logged on to the Wi-Fi?

Andreas: It wouldn't go anywhere. You have to log on first.

Coach: It's the same with all audiences. Until you "connect" to the audience, ain't nothing going anywhere.

Connect first. Send second.

All of the techniques and skills we have been teaching you to develop are simply some ways to connect to an audience: strong language; eye contact; using names; involving the audience. They don't have to take a long time, but you have to create the connection so that you can get your message through.

SUMMARY

★ Answer the questions that your audience members are thinking but do not ask, in the order in which they are not asking them.

★ Allow your audience members to interrupt you and make decisions. It will strengthen your connection with them.

CHAPTER 10

The Power of Stories

★

If history were taught in the form of stories,
it would never be forgotten.
—RUDYARD KIPLING

London, 1762, very late at night. An English nobleman, John Montagu (1718–1792), the fourth Earl of Sandwich, is hungry again, but he's too busy gambling to stop for a meal. According to legend, he orders a waiter to bring him a few slabs of roast beef between two slices of bread. The earl then goes on gambling, supplied with a snack that he can hold in his hands. He apparently had the meat put between the slices of bread so that he wouldn't get his fingers greasy while he was playing cards. From that incident, we have inherited the quick-food product that we now know as the *sandwich*.

Did you ever wonder where we got the word *sandwich*? Me neither, but now you know. If someone were to ask you next week where the word *sandwich* came from, would you be able to tell him? How much of this story would you be able to remember, and why?

We have talked a lot about language in this book—using strong language to paint pictures and evoke emotions in our audiences, and how storytelling can be an extremely powerful technique for leading our audiences where we want them to go, especially when we are opening our presentations. I'm embarrassed to admit this, but we at Own the Room didn't invent the technique of storytelling. It is one of the most ancient forms of art and a time-honored method of teaching. Great leaders throughout the ages have used storytelling to motivate, inspire, and educate their audiences. Religious leaders have taught with stories.

But, what makes a story?

A story, by definition, is just a sequence of events—fiction or non-fiction—that takes place in the past, present, or future. Of course, we all know that telling a story *well* is an art, but you can develop that art by practicing. Let's practice a little bit of the science that *supports* practicing that art well.

Stories are almost pure pictures and emotions.

The more you can *paint a picture* in the mind of the audience and *evoke emotions while you do so*, the more memorable the story becomes—the more it sticks in the memory centers of the brain.

Stories are about characters and conflict.

You've heard this formula before: boy meets girl; boy loses girl; boy gets girl. It's about characters overcoming conflict. Characters *without* conflict is not a story: "There were some nice people, and they all got along." That's not a story.

Conflict without characters is not a story. World War II is an event, but it's not a story until you tell it through the eyes of a character.

Let's examine the elements of a story.

Characters

We need to understand characters in order to make sense of a story. The more we care about the characters, the more we care about the story.

When a writer introduces a character into a book, what does she do? She describes the character's physical appearance (a picture) and personality (emotions). These help us to care about the character.

In one of our recent trainings, we were fortunate to have nationally recognized obstetrician Dr. Sonia Hassan, of Wayne State Medical in Detroit, give a presentation on the work she was doing to combat premature birth rates. She described "Zach," born at 26 weeks, weighing only a few pounds and clinging to life, his future uncertain and his parents consumed with despair and anguish. She let the conflict develop as she brought the characters to a resolution, which in this story was a happy ending.

When you are telling a story to an audience, bring your characters to life with a brief description that helps the audience visualize and respond emotionally to them.

Exercise: Pick someone in your family and describe him well in two sentences. In the first sentence, describe the person's physical appearance so that we can envision him in our minds. It doesn't have to be a complete, accurate description of what he looks like. It could be just a detail or two describing his unique features. In the second sentence, tell us about his personality.

Conflict

Think of your all-time favorite books or movies. What was the story? An underdog boxer overcoming every obstacle to beat the world champion? A young girl escaping the clutches of an evil witch to return to her farm in Kansas?

Why are reality television shows so popular with viewers? They have colorful characters, of course, but they also have characters that are *in conflict*. In business, when we are talking about our company, we often try to edit out the conflict. We want people to think that everything is wonderful and everybody gets along. But conflict is the secret ingredient of stories. If we say that our company is great and everything in the world is fine, we're not telling a very compelling story.

Conflict is a group of problems and challenges faced by the characters in a story that sets up the need for a resolution.

The human brain is wired to crave resolution. The members of your audience will not raise their filters during your story because they want to hear the resolution.

Think about this the next time you write a press release. If your release says that your institution is doing something good and all is wonderful, what is that press release lacking?

Resolution

Let's return to our friend, the Earl of Sandwich. He's the only main character in this story, but he overcame a conflict. He figured out how to satisfy his hunger without interrupting his gambling. The end of the story is the resolution of the conflict.

The characters in your story should confront a conflict or a problem, and that conflict should develop into a resolution by the end of your story. In our example, the earl invented a new dish to solve his eating/gambling dilemma, but let's say that you are trying to sell your company's new software application to potential clients. Maybe you would tell a story about an existing client who was trying to solve a very difficult problem, and how your software solved that problem for her.

Be sincere; be brief; be seated.
—FRANKLIN D. ROOSEVELT

Keep It Short

We are often asked, "How long is a good story?" Most people in business use up to twice as many words as they really need in order to say something. They take two minutes to tell a one-minute story. Once you get a story down to the right time, you will know. There is no exact right time. When is a movie too long or too short? When is a song too long or too short? A well-told story captures our attention, but a story that drags on begins to raise filters. No matter how intriguing your story is, if it goes on for too long, you will begin to lose your audience.

SUMMARY

★ Stories are about characters who overcome a conflict. Bring your story to a resolution.

★ When introducing characters, provide a brief description of their physical features and personality traits so that your audience will remember them.

★ Stories are one of the most powerful ways to paint pictures and evoke emotions.

Practice:

Think of a favorite person or pet. How would you describe him or her? What does she look like? How does he laugh? Describe the person for one minute to a coworker, family member, or friend. Videotape it.

Now, think of a time of crisis or conflict in your own life. Practice telling that story aloud in one minute. Videotape yourself telling the story. Do not go over one minute.

Review your videos. Play them back, demand feedback, and delete the evidence.

CHAPTER 11

Yes, You Are . . . Funny!

You have two ears and one mouth.
Use them proportionately.
—EPICTETUS

I f you have access to the Internet, let's do something a little different for this chapter. I want you to pick a funny joke. You can search for one on your own, or just pick one of the ones that we have compiled for you at http://www.owntheroom.com/training/jokes. It's a list of dozens of preapproved funny jokes on the Internet that are *clean.* (So, you won't know any of them.)

Go ahead and read a couple, then pick one and memorize it.

Now share it out loud.

If you are in a public place, just turn to someone and say, "Can I tell you a joke?"

We all have different senses of humor. The people in your audience will *always* get your humor once they adjust to your personality. It just takes a few minutes for them to get to know you. But for humor to work, you have to let your personality out. You have to commit to *being you.*

During one of my early speaking engagements, while I was still a student, I was invited to travel to a private college in Chicago to receive a national award. There were a few thousand people in the audience, and at the time, the television game show *Wheel of Fortune* was popular. As I paused before beginning my acceptance speech, I looked out at the audience, took a breath, turned to the moderator, and said, "Um, can I buy a vowel if I need to?" Crickets. Not everything works, but at least I can laugh about it now!

Which brings us to the big question: Should you start your presentations with a joke?

The prospect of trying to be funny and failing or having a joke not work terrifies people, but humor is one of the most wonderful and effective forms of communication in a speaker's toolbox. Jokes, stories, teasing the audience, letting the audience tease you—these are all techniques that you can weave through your presentation to drop your audience's filters and connect with its members in a very human way.

You definitely want to use as much humor as you can. The secret is to use it when it makes sense. Many people tell me that they wish they could tell jokes. Trust me, anyone can tell a joke. Most people can't remember the joke. This is what causes a joke to fall flat. You cannot possibly focus on how to tell the joke—timing, rhythm, and delivery—if you are trying to remember it. If you are going to use a joke in your presentation, your first step is to commit it to memory. This is the lesson taught by the great philosopher Marlin. (Nemo's dad, the clownfish, in the movie *Finding Nemo*.)

The next step in perfecting a joke is to practice your delivery. Watch some videos of your favorite comedians and notice their technique. You will find very little weak language, and a great use of pauses. These comedians have practiced their performances over and over again, and they're enjoying what they're doing while they're doing it.

What do you have to get right to tell a joke well? Everything. One of the most perfect forms of communication we humans have is a story, and one of the most perfect forms of a story is a joke.

Great comedians also base their material on what *they* find funny. They notice something about everyday life that amuses them.

"Why do we drive on parkways and park in driveways?"

They then perfect the art of sharing their amusement with the audience by practicing their timing, tone, and body language. Because of mirror neurons, the audience shares the comedian's amusement and finds what he is saying to be funny. When you're working humor into your presentations, start with what *you* find funny and laugh *with* the audience.

College students are more likely to remember a statistical lecture when the professor includes relevant jokes about the topic.

Like many of the people who have attended my training sessions, Ann, a marketing vice president with a major firm, shared her personal horror story of trying, unsuccessfully, to start her presentation with a joke:

Ann: I tried to start with a joke once, and they didn't laugh.

Coach: So what did you do?

Ann: I just went back to normal speaking and didn't try to be funny. And I tried to cover up how embarrassed I was. But I'm not sure it worked.

Coach: One reason an audience doesn't laugh, and this is normal, is because they don't know you yet. They aren't expecting you to be joking. They just don't know how funny you are!

Comedians have a big advantage over the rest of us because we know they are comedians. Before they even say a word, we are expecting humor; we are ready to laugh. For the rest of us, it requires a little transition. This is especially true if you have a dry sense of humor. It takes at least a couple of references before people recognize and appreciate your style. You can't lose confidence before that appreciation kicks in. Next time, either let them know that a joke is coming or just keep going with another one, and you will see a difference.

What Is Not So Funny

Here's a conversation that occurred during a training in Dubai:

Himanshu: What do you think of ethnic jokes?

Coach: Uh-oh, here we go. What do *you* think of them?

Sauro: They can get you in trouble, but they *can* be very funny.

Coach: Agreed. So know your audience and be careful. When you offend someone, the person you offended could keep her filters up for a long time. We've all heard of people in business who put down women with a little remark here or there. Don't think it goes unnoticed. The same is true of comments about any minority. It's also true of cursing. Some people hate it; some don't mind; some like it; some find it entertaining. But the ones that hate it can associate you with it for a long time.

Coach: What is the one safe group you can make fun of?

Roland: Americans!

Coach: Hey, watch it. (*smiling*)

Alex: Your own.

Coach: (*turning to Alex and bowing*) Well spoken, young Padawan. Listen to Alex, everyone. You can make fun of your "own group." Men can make fun of men. Catholics can make fun of Catholics. Dutch people can make fun of Dutch people. But when you tease other people and groups, be very careful, or just make it the opposite of a backhanded compliment. Make it a tease that actually makes them look good.

With jokes that target a specific group of people, it is crucially important that you know your audience very well, and that you are very careful. When you offend someone, the person you offended can keep his filters up for a very long time. He won't hear or remember anything else you say.

I have seen speakers casually make fun of gays, Republicans, and Democrats for no apparent reason or gain, just trying to be funny. Some of these jokes did get some laughs, but trust me, the people who were turned off will *stay* turned off. Sexual orientation, race, ethnicity, gender, politics, religion—these are personal issues. You do not want to risk offense with jokes about certain groups of people. Even if I am not a member of a group, I can be offended by your offending them.

Let's use politics as an example. Unless you are speaking at the Democratic or Republican convention, be careful with putting down or ridiculing other political views just to be funny. I guarantee you that in almost any audience, there will be people who are politically more to the left or the right than you would assume or guess. (And, should you be addressing a political convention, as some of my clients have, do remember that most of the people watching you at home on television are independents.) You cannot assume that you know the political, religious, or social views of your audience. Why turn off your audience for no reason or benefit?

The one possible exception to this rule is when you make fun of yourself or your "own group," but you must still be very careful. This type of delicate humor requires particular skill, and can easily backfire, with unfortunate effects.

Another type of humor where people often unintentionally undercut themselves is in using self-deprecating humor. Again, making fun of yourself can be a very effective way of connecting with your audience, but you don't want to cross the line into undermining your own authority or competence.

In attempting to use humor, here are examples of phrases you *never* want to say:

I need to bore you with some logistics. Even though you are joking, you don't want them to ever associate the word *boring* with you.

If I had more time, I would go into . . . Don't make excuses. Fit your content to the time you have.

I am really nervous right now. It's nice to be authentic and open, but it's outweighed by putting all the focus on *you*—away from the audience.

I didn't pick this joke. You are qualifying and undercutting yourself before you start.

SUMMARY

★ Humor is one of the most effective tools in the speaker's toolbox. Don't be afraid to use it.

★ Give your audience members the chance to realize that you are funny. It may take a few jokes before they get it.

★ Memorize a joke before you tell it to an audience. Most people who fall flat do so because they are struggling to remember the joke.

★ Avoid jokes that make fun of individual groups of people or involve sensitive topics like politics and religion.

Practice

Select a joke that makes you laugh. Memorize it. Practice telling the joke to your family, friends, or coworkers. Work on your timing and tone. Once it gets a good laugh, you have it down for life. Over time, add to your repertoire.

CHAPTER 12

Finding Your Own Style

★

*Each second we live is a new and unique moment of the universe,
a moment that will never be again. And what do we teach our
children? We teach them that two and two make four and that
Paris is the capital of France. When will we also teach them what
they are? We should say to each of them: Do you know what you
are? You are a marvel. You are unique. In all the years that have
passed, there has never been another child like you.*
—PABLO PICASSO

I am often asked in coaching, "What does it take to get really good?
How good am I, and how do I get to a higher level?" On a scale of
zero to ten, I would rate most speakers I meet in business at about a
four. Not bad, but not good. The same as I was when I started originally. They coast on their talent and intelligence and have had very little
actual training. But, there is much more potential in them.

Improving from a four to a six is relatively simple. Most people
can make that leap with a good 25-hour training course. Improving
from a six to an eight takes a greater investment of time and training, including working in front of a camera, additional coaching, and
opening your mind to embrace, not just hear, feedback.

Beyond that, to get from an eight to a ten, either you've got it or
you don't. Most people assume that personality and charisma are the

key factors in being a great speaker or presenter. Charisma *is* part of effective speaking, but only part of it. The true power of public speaking, the stuff that gets you invited into the Olympics of presenters, is the ability to *read* an audience. Once you learn how to read an audience's eyes and body language, there is no limit to how good you can get. If you can read a person one-on-one, you can learn to read an audience.

The great artist Pablo Picasso became famous because of his very distinctive style, which took common objects and forms, including the human body, and represented them in highly altered ways. As much as Picasso can teach us about the power of our own individuality and uniqueness, and the necessity of marshaling that power to stand out, he can also teach us a much more useful lesson about connecting with an audience.

Close your eyes and imagine a human face. Do not look at any pictures or people; just imagine a face. In terms of a fraction, how far down from the top of the head are the eyes?

Most people say one-fourth or one-third of the way down the face, when they are actually located halfway. On every human face they are exactly halfway between the top of the head and bottom of the chin—directly in the middle of the head (the hairline throws us off).*

The problem with our early drawings was not that we couldn't draw. The problem was that we couldn't *see*. Even though, as children, we had seen thousands of faces, we didn't see them in their proper proportions. We correctly drew what we incorrectly saw. This is why most people think they can't draw. Not knowing that the problem is our inability to see, we give up, thinking we don't have the ability or the talent to draw. To learn how to draw, first you must learn how to see.

Artists know this. They also know that they can't just draw what they see. Sometimes they draw what they don't see. They use shadows and shading to create mood, or the illusion of an object.

---

*Bob Davies, How to Draw and Paint, PaintBox Art Media, Ltd., www.how-to-draw -and-paint.com.

Our art teacher eventually teaches us not only where to place the eyes, but that the distance between our two eyes is equal to a third eye, that the top of the ears is level with the eyes, and that the bottom of the nose is two-fifths of the way from the eyes to the chin.

Speaking works the same way. Before you can learn how to speak, you must first learn how to *hear*. You must learn how to *hear* what makes an audience's filters go up, and what makes them go down. You learn to hear what parts of your presentation become memorable for your audiences, and what parts they are not retaining. You must learn to hear the beauty of silence, and how to communicate without speaking. To unleash your own ability, you need to hear the patterns of response that indicate that your presentation is working, so that you can create things that your audience has not yet seen. You must learn to hear what the people in your audience are telling you through their eyes, body language, and other verbal and nonverbal clues. The ability to convey to those in your audience that you "hear" them can be a form of charisma. It's also a skill that you can develop and a technique that you can use very effectively, regardless of your natural charisma.

Natural Charisma

Good news! Not only can you create charisma by learning to read your audience, but yes, you do have your own natural charisma. Everybody does. Charisma is your ability to make your audience members feel good about themselves. Most people don't know how much charisma they have simply because they've never developed it enough to find out.

Imagine that your laptop battery has died, and you need to charge it. You attach the power cord to the computer and plug it into the wall outlet. An hour later, when you try to use your computer, it still won't boot up. Why? You check, and you realize that the cord had fallen out of the outlet. The cord has to be plugged in on both ends for the computer to charge.

It's the same with charisma. Your authentic personality is the cord transmitting your message to the audience. When you make that connection, that's when the energy flows. But, it has to be plugged in at both ends. Rule of thumb: Presentations should be customized at both ends. Your presentation style and goals, and the audience's presentation style and goals.

Charisma is just the starting point, though. It's the way you create your connection to the audience so that your message can be delivered. It is possible to have charisma—which we can also think of as real presence—and not deliver content, so we have to be careful about placing too much emphasis on sheer personality. If an audience can't remember anything from a presentation, but thought the speaker was great, that might be an example of a charismatic speaker who didn't deliver much value. That can be all of us at times. Then there are perhaps less naturally charismatic speakers whose audience remembered their message because they used effective techniques to deliver their content successfully.

Back to our laptop. If you want to charge up your audience with your charisma, you have to express your personality and make that connection with your audience in an inspiring way.

One of the most effective ways to connect with your audience is, simply, to be yourself. Although you can learn something useful and important from every speaker you hear, there is only one style that will ever fit *you: your style is perfect for you*. Your perfect presentation is *you* being perfectly *you*, connecting perfectly with the audience. Trying to mimic or copy someone else's presentation style is a tactical error that will only produce disappointing results. It will never be authentic. Each of us is unique; we cannot be duplicated. The only style that will ever be effective for you is *your own*.

Often, the way we come across to our friends, family, or colleagues when we are excited, passionate, or focused gets lost when we make an official presentation. I see this all of the time. Share your passion for your content, and let your personality shine through. If you don't have any passion for the topic you are presenting, maybe it's time to ask yourself why you are presenting it.

People used to say, you can't be emotional in business. Especially you, women: don't be emotional!

That's ridiculous. Most business is emotion, but you have to access appropriate emotions at the appropriate times. Confidence, strength, hope, excitement, frustration—these are all emotions that, if we can convey them to and inspire them in our audience, can make our presentations extremely effective. Not only can you be emotional, but you have to be. In fact, research has shown that 80 percent of business decisions are made emotionally.* This doesn't mean that there is no logic as the basis for the decision, but the final decision? Buy or don't buy? That's largely emotional.

Just make sure that the emotion you want your audience to feel is the one that you're sending.

I've learned in coaching that some people feel, for a variety of reasons, that it's not safe for them to "be themselves" at work. Another way to think of it is as being your "appropriate" self. You are being the "real you," but appropriate to the context. To become a great speaker, you must get better and better at being your true and best self—in a way that is appropriate to the situation.

Some people interpret that last statement to mean "just be yourself." That is the root of the theory, but the part about being "appropriate to the situation" is just as important. You can be passionate when you're pitching an idea to the boss at work, and be just as passionate when you're discussing your political opinions with a friend. But that doesn't mean that you should be expressing your political views to your boss or making your friend listen to your sales pitch. What is appropriate in one situation is not appropriate in the other, but in both situations, you are being authentic, the real you, your true and best self.

World-class speakers sometimes make mistakes, large and small, in their presentations all the time. Do you want to know what their secret is for not becoming flustered or thrown off by mistakes?

They don't care.

---

*Dan Hill, *Emotionomics: Leveraging Emotions for Business Success* (London: Kogan Page, Ltd., 2010).

They don't care.

Most people never notice when a great speaker makes a mistake because the speakers themselves don't care. They know that it's not about them. They are focused on the audience and the delivery. A great speaker does not let himself be held back by the need to be perfect the way that need holds back others. Great speakers aren't worried about whether they look good. They worry about whether their audience is having a good experience. How you view mistakes says more about you than it says about the mistakes. A speaker is good when she is herself and she delivers an important message or helps her audience get something meaningful. It doesn't matter whether your technique is perfect, whether you make mistakes, or whether you are extremely entertaining. All that matters is that your audience gets what you want it to get.

Andre Agassi, in addition to his skills on the tennis court and in the boardroom (he is doing amazing work with charter schools), is also one of the best storytellers I know, and he told me, "We're all swimming to Hawaii, and none of us is going to make it. Keep swimming anyway."

I think of this as it relates to mastering anything, like communication, that is not truly masterable. There is no upper limit to how good you can get. There is always more to learn. To quote the smiling Dory in *Finding Nemo*, "Just keep swimming." (You can see how old my kids are.) Enjoy the journey.

SUMMARY

★ Charisma is your ability to connect your authentic personality with the audience's personality. Everyone has charisma.

★ The key to becoming a great presenter is to get better and better at being your best, true, authentic self in a way that is appropriate to the situation.

★ Never try to copy someone else. Your own style is the perfect style for you.

★ Great speakers don't care about making mistakes. Mistakes help you learn and improve, and your audience won't care that you made them.

★ Showing emotion can be extremely effective in public speaking. Let the people in your audience see your passion for your topic, and they will feel it, too.

CHAPTER 13

———

Make It Special

★

If you don't know what you want to achieve in
your presentation, your audience never will.
—Harvey Diamond

There is a term in economics called *discretionary income*. It is the amount of money from your paycheck that is left over after you pay all your bills. Once you have paid for your mortgage or rent, utilities, groceries, car, and other necessities, discretionary income is what's left over to buy new clothes or go on a vacation. You can spend this money any way you want. It's at your discretion.

For the purpose of our individual careers, let's make up a term called *discretionary effort*. Each of us has a certain amount of work we have to do to perform our job. We are capable of accomplishing much more when we want to—when we are motivated. It is at our discretion to find and give that extra effort.

A frequent question during our training sessions is, "What can I do to make my presentations special?"

I usually respond to this question with a wonderful exercise that I learned from my friend Cory Booker, New Jersey's new U.S. senator. He didn't invent it, and we know that Facebook's Sheryl Sandberg used it long before he did, but none of us knows who invented it. But it works, so here we go.

Hold this book in one hand, and with your free hand, reach up as high as you can.

Now reach three centimeters higher.

Wait a minute! I said, "as high as you can" the first time.

If you are like most people, you were able to find those extra three centimeters. Where did you find them? Even when you thought you had already reached as high as you could, you found that you had more in you. You could reach higher, and it wasn't that hard to do.

More important question: *Why* did you reach an extra three centimeters?

You did it simply because I asked.

Most people think the power of leadership is making brilliant statements, but the real power of leadership is sometimes *asking powerful short questions*.

We all make brilliant statements from time to time, but power also comes from asking simple questions.

There is always more in you. Now it is your job to ask yourself: "What can I do to reach another few centimeters, to make it different or special?"

Regardless of how polished or rough around the edges you are at this point in your speaking career, there is always room to grow. No one can ever reach his full potential in a field like communications because there is always more to do. There is no upper limit; your potential is limitless.

Those three extra centimeters are the difference between good and great—in communication, in life, or in just about any endeavor that you attempt. A few percentage points can be the difference between a number one and a number two market share. A few seconds can be the difference between an Olympic gold medal and not even making the finals.

In the long run, men hit only what they aim at.
Therefore, they better hit at something high.
—HENRY DAVID THOREAU

When you are preparing your presentations, you need to sit back and think, "What can I do to make this a little different, to give it more impact? What could provide that extra *oomph*? What would make my presentation stand out?"

Every time you see something work for somebody else in a meeting or a presentation, file it away in your memory until you have the chance to try it. Maybe it will work for you and maybe it won't. Who cares? Risk taking and being willing to test your creativity are part of those three extra centimeters. When a new technique or idea works for you a few times, it will become part of your toolbox for building great presentations.

> You don't own these techniques by learning them. You're just renting them. You own new techniques after you do them a few times in front of a live audience and they work.

Many of the executives I coach are very no-nonsense, cut-to-the-chase, get-to-the-bottom-line types of people. They like what they're hearing during training, but they want a solution for improving their presentations that is quick and to the point. Andrew, a friend, approached me during a training once and asked me to give him *just one tip* to improve his meetings.

Coach: One tip?

Andrew: Yes. What is the number one tip that can make my meetings better?

Coach: Do something different at each and every meeting.

Andrew: Just one thing?

continued

Coach: Especially at the openings. How did you open your last meeting?

Andrew: I went through the agenda.

Coach: Okay, so that is off the table now, and you have to start your next meeting with something different. What could you do to open your next meeting?

Andrew: I like the thing about starting with a story.

Coach: Perfect. Pick a story that relates to your agenda and start with that the next time. Then, for your next meeting after that, that opening will be off the table. So, how do you open that meeting?

Andrew: (*thinking*) I could start with a question.

Coach: After a few weeks, you won't have to continue thinking of something new. You can begin to recycle them. Save the planet.

If you do something different each time you conduct a meeting or give a presentation, the people in your audience will become more engaged. They will start to look for what you are going to do next, and they will arrive at the meeting interested and enthusiastic. Their filters will be down even before you start to speak.

You have to take risks and push boundaries. Of course, by its very definition, a risk can backfire or not work out well. When you introduce a new technique into your presentation, you must be prepared for it to feel awkward and uncomfortable at first. It will take some time before it feels natural. The first time you pass a prop around, for example, it just may not go well. You will get subtle signals from your audience that the technique is not working, or you may get a look that says, "Cute, but let's not do that again."

That is not a reason to give up. You can figure out why the technique didn't work and make adjustments or adaptations, but do not abandon it. Fine-tune it, practice it, and work out the kinks, but don't just stop. Soon you will have a reputation for being creative, professional, and very effective in your communication.

If you are worried that a new technique won't work the first time you try it, I can magically remove that worry. Often, it doesn't work. You feel uncomfortable, and the technique doesn't land right. This is one of the big advantages of attending a training class, either in person or online. A couple of repetitions and you will have it down, so that when you do it in real life, you stick that landing.

> There's no such thing as trying too hard. People who try to do too much right away and try too hard to do techniques that they are not quite mastering are the ones who progress the fastest. It's okay to make mistakes, and it's okay to make those mistakes faster.

Be constantly on the lookout for that delicate balance between professionalism and innovation; structure and creativity; results and process. Trust your instincts, and be faster to act on them. Here again, I like to use the analogy of rowing a boat. You need to have two oars in the water. If you have only one oar moving, you will go in circles. If you have structure, but you don't get people thinking creatively, you will go in circles and never move forward. If you get people thinking creatively, but you don't have structure, you will circle in the other direction. You need both if you are to move forward.

Many of the techniques, tools, and skills that we need if we are to be effective in our public speaking and communication are applicable to being an effective leader and, perhaps most important, to our lives in general. The world does not give you permission to be your full and best self. Most people are like fast sports cars driven with the hand brake on. Release your brake. "But, what if I hit the curb?"

Our senior coach, Mikkel Kloster, gave this tune-up to a race car named John:

John: I really love all the stuff we've learned today, but I am a bit worried that I won't be able to use it all.

Mikkel: Worried?

John: Yeah, the techniques really make sense, but when I'm in the situation, I am worried I will forget them and go back to my old ways.

Mikkel: Why do you think that?

John: It's all new! And there's so much to think about. When I'm in the situation, I don't feel like I have time to get it exactly right because I need to think about it. And then I lose the moment.

Mikkel: How important is it to get it, as you say, "exactly right"?

John: Well . . . (*thinking*) . . . I guess it doesn't have to be perfectly textbook all of the time.

Mikkel: Why not?

John: I guess I would be the only one in the room who would care about that.

Mikkel: What would the others in the room be caring about?

John: I guess they would just be happy if my presentation is less boring than what they normally experience.

Mikkel: I think you're right. And if you worry too much about getting it exactly right, who are you thinking about? You or the audience?

John: Myself! I know what you're going to say now. I should be thinking about the audience! Got the point.

Mikkel: It was *your* point. The trick to learning all these techniques is not to try and master everything at once. Pick out a few that you really like. Work on those on any given occasion. Within a few weeks you will own them for life. Then pick out a couple of other ones. Focusing on many things at the same time is bad for learning. Better to learn one thing at a time, then the next, then the next.

Do you know how to drive a car?

John: Sure!

Mikkel: How did it feel the first time you got behind the wheel?

John: Like there were way too many things to think about at the same time! Pedals, signals, traffic signs, other cars, you name it!

Mikkel: How does it feel now to get behind the wheel?

John: I can get in my car, turn on the radio, and suddenly realize I am at work!

Mikkel: Why do you think that is?

John: Well, of course, because I've done it so much, that now it feels natural and I just do it.

Mikkel: You are right. And the techniques you've learned today are like a car. To use them you must consciously think about them. It doesn't feel natural, it's not automated—yet! If you make the decision that you want to own these techniques, you want to become a better speaker and you want it to feel natural—you can get there. Now you have the car. It's up to you if you want to drive it, or just leave it in the garage.

John: Hmmm . . . (*smiling.*) I would hate having an awesome car and then just let it sit in the garage. I want to drive it!

Hit some curbs. You will recover.

There is no secret conspiracy to hold you back, but there might as well be, because it works like one. The resistance you encounter is a mile wide but an inch thick. Break through. Communication is about leadership, and leadership is about courage. The more you do something—in this case, the more you work to constantly improve your presentations—the easier it will get.

The world generally stops caring about your development when you finish school. When we are in school, we have parents, teachers, and professors who instruct and correct us, but when our formal schooling is done, that support can come to a sudden, if not obvious, end. It is as if the world says, "This one is finished. Release it into the wild!"

Now you have to be the CEO of your own potential; the Dean of your own classes, semester and degrees in life skills you want. You have to chart your own course for learning. You have to be assertive and dedicated to make happen for yourself what you want to have happen. Do you want to become a good dancer or learn a new computer application, sport, or language? You can do it, and you have many options available to you for accomplishing it, but you have to make it happen. You have to take the initiative.

Occasionally, we are lucky enough to have a friend, boss, or company that creates structured learning opportunities for us, so that we can grow. We should be grateful for these opportunities, but they are rare. If you are waiting for the world to see your potential and chart a path for you, or if you think that the jungle is going to open up and a yellow brick road is going to form just for you, you may have a very long wait. You must choose your own destination, and then forge your path yourself.

The next time you feel that the world is not giving you permission to be your full self, what should you do? The answer is simple: be brilliant anyway. You do not need a letter from Mom pinned to your shirt reminding you to be brilliant, but here's one from motivational speaker and author Marianne Williams:

> Our deepest fear is not that we are inadequate. Our deepest fear is that we are powerful beyond measure. It is our light, not our darkness, that most frightens us. We ask ourselves, "Who am I to be brilliant, gorgeous, talented, fabulous?" Actually, who are you not to be? You are a child of God. Your playing small does not serve the world. There is nothing enlightened about shrinking so that other people won't feel insecure around you. We are all meant to shine, as children do. We were born to make manifest the glory of God that is within us. It's not just in some of us; it's in everyone.

Who are you to be brilliant? Who are you not to be?

SUMMARY

★ Always reach for those three extra centimeters. Ask yourself, what can I do to make this presentation different? How can I make it special?

★ If you do something different each time you give a presentation, you will build a reputation for being a dynamic speaker, and the people in your audience will arrive with their filters down.

★ Take responsibility for your own growth and improvement, and give yourself permission to be brilliant. The world is not going to give it to you.

★ Notice little things, and try new things.

SUMMARY

PART III

MAKING THE *AUDIENCE* THE STAR

Our greatest hits for keeping the crowd on its feet:

★ Audience involvement techniques

★ Great openings with *imagine*

★ Closings that bring commitment

★ Memorable team presentations

CHAPTER 14

Involve the Audience: Wave of the Future

*No man would listen to you talk if he
didn't know it was his turn next.*

—E. W. HOWE

A t this point, if you were to take all the techniques you have learned so far and incorporate them confidently into your presentations, you would find a dramatic change in your ability to connect with and influence your audience, and in your dynamism as a speaker. You would definitely feel, and accurately so, that you had ratcheted up your original rating as a speaker by several points.

We have learned how the brain sends and receives information; how and why our audience blocks out our message; how to connect with our audience and lower its filters; and how to modulate our voices, employ body language, and use the room. We have learned to eliminate weak language; to use strong language to paint pictures, set scenes, and evoke emotions; and to craft strong openings. All of these techniques provide us with a strong and solid foundation upon which we can build our presentations.

Now it's time to reach for those extra three centimeters and, as a famous chef likes to say, kick things up a notch. Let's think for a moment. What could you possibly do, as a presenter, that would just about guarantee that the people in your audience would remain focused on you and engaged in your presentation, listening to your every word?

Make them active participants in your presentation. Now we go from *just you* being a star, to making the audience the star.

Communication can be aggressive, passive, or assertive.
Poor communication often creates
tension and bad feelings within relationships.

We have already learned one technique for making our audience the star: allowing them to make decisions. There are several other very effective techniques for making your audience an active part of your presentation.

Around the Room

Go around the room and ask each person to offer an opinion on your subject, or to give an answer to a question that you pose.

This starter thought can be a very useful opening technique. At the very top of your presentation, ask each person to share a one-sentence thought on the topic you are about to discuss.

Going around the room can be very effective at *any* point in the presentation: "I want to walk you through three strategies, and then ask each of you to share in one sentence which strategy you think is the greatest priority for our company and why."

The around the room technique accomplishes several objectives. It engages everyone emotionally in the topic, it drops filters, it gives the presenter *and* the rest of the audience data about the audience members' opinions on the topic, and it gives the presenter a break, time to think ahead.

Body Polls

Most people know standard ways to engage your audience, like conducting a poll.

"Raise your hand if you have kids."

"How many people here are from out of town?"

Standard polls like these are good, but they are binary questions, meaning that there are only two possible answers; they don't require too much thought or inspire too much creativity.

Body polls use body parts to query the audience with a *range* of answers falling on a spectrum. Participants are asked to indicate their answers by using, perhaps, a body part that harmonizes with the question.

For example:

Show me with your fingers, on a scale from zero to ten, how concerned you are about climate change. Ten means, "I can't sleep at night worrying about it," and zero means, "Not one bit."

Or:

Show me with your thumb which direction you think the economy is headed over the next five years: straight up means through the roof, straight down means the opposite, level means stays exactly the same, or anywhere in between.

Another example:

Stand up. When I say "go," act out, with your body language, your favorite vacation activity—swimming, skiing, hiking, sleeping. If you see someone who appears to be acting out the same activity as you, move toward that person.

Body polls are a lot of fun, create a lot of energy, and mark you as a creative and different speaker. Most importantly, they can be used for silly or serious purposes because they collect a lot of data quickly. They can be straightforward, like the first two examples, or they can be wildly creative, like the third example, with plenty of room in between. You can use body polls throughout your presentation by simply changing the question and the body language you want the people in your audience to use to indicate their answers.

Again, a body poll is providing you with data about your audience. Once you have these data, you must react to them *somehow*. If you put your audience through a body poll and then just move on to something else, people will wonder about the purpose of the poll and begin to think that this really fun, creative idea was pointless and wasted their time. They will question why you polled them and why they had to perform the exercise. The filters that the body poll lowered so effectively will be on the rise.

Think of the data as clay. You have to build something with the clay. Do something with the data generated by the body poll. Ask for or point out the average opinion in the room. Point out the outliers—the people whose answers formed the extreme deviations from the norm—and ask them about their answers. Make a comment or a joke. Allow the audience to make its own observations. We get asked a lot how to bring more humor into presentations. Half of your humor can come from the audience by creating opportunities like this.

Of course, your body poll question should be related to the topic of your presentation. If you use the data your audience provided to strengthen or illustrate the next point you are about to make, the people in your audience will feel that they assisted you, and they will feel good about this. Their filters will be down.

Here are some examples of body polls, ranging from serious to creative, that our participants created during our classes:

> Looking at this investment opportunity, show me with your feet, what you think we should do. Stand by this wall if you think we need to sign the term sheet now. Stand by the opposite wall if you

think we should stay far away from this opportunity. Or, stand anywhere in between. Now, tell me over here, why you think we shouldn't invest. Over here, tell us why we should.

Show me with your smartphone, way up here being the highest, down by your knees the lowest, how much you, ten years ago, used your smartphone for banking and finance (most were very low). Five years ago? One year ago? Now? Three years from now? Based on that trend, what should our business be doing?

Show me with your fingers how many devices you can think of that you use on a regular basis that had not yet been *invented* when you started high school. Okay, let's go around the room and each say one of them.

Let's make this room a map of the world. Up there is north, where Santa Claus lives. This is North America here. Everyone point to New York City. Good. Point to Los Angeles. South America. Europe. Asia. Okay, now everyone go to the place in the room where your mother's, mother's, mother was born.

Body polls are a simple but powerful technique, but like all the techniques we will learn in this book, they are just raw techniques until you infuse them with your own ideas and personality. As the previous examples show, the technique doesn't really come alive until then.

My friend Joi Ito, director of the MIT media lab, went through our training and said he liked the body poll concept, but he kept forgetting (or chickening out, he said) to use it in his presentations. Then he e-mailed me a link and said he did his first body poll, in front of 4,000 people, and it went great. It's easier to show you than tell you, so let's do Joi's body poll together now.

Show me with your fingers, with 10 being the highest, how good an artist you *thought* you were when you were four years old. Ten means you thought you were great at art. Go. (The average in the group was pretty high.) Now show me how good an artist you think you are *today*. (The average was now pretty low.)

Joi then asked the group, "What happened?"

The point Joi was making about how our attitudes change as we get older is brilliant, but by flipping it into a body poll and involving the audience in making that point, he makes it more personal, and more powerful. When the body poll is done, pivot to your next section.

Assign Jobs

You can engage your audience very effectively by assigning audience members specific jobs or roles in your presentation. Some of these jobs can be assigned at the start of your presentation, while others can be assigned during the course of the presentation. Some jobs to consider are:

Timekeeper

Recorder

Prop holder

Subject of a demonstration

Participant in a role-playing exercise

When individuals do a task or job for you, thank them. Thanks is their pay. In real life when we work, our employers pay us. If they don't pay us, we all get cranky. When individuals volunteer for you, your thanks is their pay. Offer small thanks for small tasks (head nod and thanking them by name), and bigger thanks for bigger tasks.

For example, let's say you have 1,000 people in the audience and you want to do a group exercise. You say, "When I say go, but not till I say go, everyone form into groups, five people in a group. Whoever's birthday is closest to today is the team captain, and you have x time to do y task." When the exercise is finished, say, "Let's give a round of applause to all the captains."

Note Cards/Sticky Notes

Hand out sticky notes and markers to the people in your audience, pose a question to them, and have them write an answer to that question in large, bold letters on the sticky notes. You can then have your audience members either group themselves by similar responses or form arbitrary groups and decide among themselves which is the best answer in the group. Finally, have audience members stick their notes on a board in the front of the room or another central location. Use the answers as a jumping-off point for discussion.

One- and Two-Word Check-Ins

This is a variation of going around the room. Ask your audience a question that people can answer in one word. For example: "Say the first word that pops into your head when you think of your last vacation." Then go around the room and have each person give his answer. As each person shares his response, he is engaged in your presentation. This technique can be used at any point in the presentation:

"If you think about PowerPoint presentations, what is the first word that comes to your mind?" Good? Bad? Ugly? Whatever word comes to mind. We are not judging.

The key to this technique is encouraging your audience members to answer. Assure them that there are no right or wrong answers. Persuade them to be honest. Make them feel safe. Observe their body language and their eyes to make sure that they understand the question.

"I am going to go around the room, and I want you to say the first word that comes to mind when you think of today's topic. I am going to start with Judy in one second, and we'll move around the room very quickly. There are no right or wrong answers. Just say the one word that pops into your head. Okay? Judy?" Give her a second to answer, and then move on to the next person. "Bill?"

Even in a group of 20 people, a one- or two-word check-in takes only a minute, but the technique allows you to accomplish those same important objectives in that short period of time:

> It involves everyone in the audience. People can't *not* participate.

> It drops filters. People have to drop them in order to answer the question.

People hear, and are influenced by, what the other audience members are saying.

It gives you, the presenter, data on what your audience is thinking. And, audience members get data from one another.

It gives you the opportunity to focus on reading people's body language.

It gives you a break, time to take a sip or think of what you are going to do or say next.

Pair Up

For this technique, the speaker pairs audience members into teams of two (or another number) and assigns them a thought-through task. In our training sessions, we will sometimes assign each group a topic or ask each group to choose a topic, then have the groups prepare a one-minute presentation or a 60-second commercial on their assigned or chosen subject. Establish the parameters of the task, such as the length of time, before you define the task, or the teams will be off and running to complete the task and will not hear the parameters.

When the time allotted for the task is up, have each team present to or share with the whole group. You can do the pair-up technique with groups larger than two. I like to mix it up, sometimes with groups of three, four, or five people.

For practicing presentations, we do a drill called "Star, Coach, Paparazzi." The audience divides into groups of three, and each group has an iPad. Each person in the group takes a turn as the star, the paparazzi, and the coach. The "star" does a 30-second presentation on topic X. The "paparazzi" films the star. The "coach" provides feedback to the star. After the star has given her presentation, the paparazzi plays it back, and the coach gives the star tips on what the star did well, what she could build on, and how she could do better. (Paparazzi can give comments too.) The "star" then does a second take, followed by a second round of feedback during playback to note improvements. The group switches roles until each person in the group has had a turn as "star," "paparazzi," and "coach."

For this particular exercise, the ideal number for a team is three, but in general, teams and groups can be any size. We have found that two-person teams are the most effective, because this format maximizes the amount of time that the team members will be speaking, listening, and participating in the task. With a two-person team, you eliminate the nonparticipation option.

Around the Room at the End of the Meeting

This technique is similar to the starter thought, but used at the end of a presentation. Pose a final question to your audience, and ask each participant, as you go around the room, to offer an answer. While starter thoughts are often used to gauge feelings and emotions, the closing question should center on action.

> "What is one hope you have for what this project will accomplish for the client?"

> "What is one thing you will do to help the plan we have developed succeed?"

> "Name one thing you commit to do based on what we discussed."

None of these audience involvement techniques require much time or preparation, yet by using them, you can involve your audience in your presentation several times even in just a few minutes.

I am from Michigan, but I have been living in New Jersey for more than 20 years because I fell in love with a Jersey girl and have been trapped here ever since. A couple of years ago, a freak snowstorm hit two days before Halloween. The trees—which are usually dry and bare by the time snow arrives—were still lush with fall foliage, and they collapsed under the weight of the snow, taking the power lines down with them. The streets of my town were ensnared in a maze of electric wires, forcing police to cancel Halloween trick-or-treating and leaving much of the area without power for several days. Until the utility crews could get those electric wires off the ground and back up on their poles, life pretty much ground to a halt.

Think of your presentation as those electric cables and the audience involvement techniques we have learned throughout this book as the poles that keep the wires up in the air. If one of those poles is missing at the proper interval, or if the poles are spaced too far apart, the cables will sag or fall to the ground. This is also true of your audience's attention. It will sag and lag if it is not propped up at regular intervals. You must continuously employ different techniques throughout your presentation to keep the audience engaged.

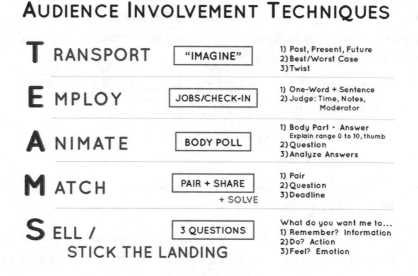

AUDIENCE INVOLVEMENT TECHNIQUES

T RANSPORT — "IMAGINE" — 1) Past, Present, Future 2) Best/Worst Case 3) Twist

E MPLOY — JOBS/CHECK-IN — 1) One-Word + Sentence 2) Judge: Time, Notes, Moderator

A NIMATE — BODY POLL — 1) Body Part - Answer Explain range 0 to 10, thumb 2) Question 3) Analyze Answers

M ATCH — PAIR + SHARE + SOLVE — 1) Pair 2) Question 3) Deadline

S ELL / STICK THE LANDING — 3 QUESTIONS — What do you want me to... 1) Remember? Information 2) Do? Action 3) Feel? Emotion

Once the people in your audience realize that you are going to be engaging them actively in your presentation, their filters will remain down as they anticipate the next exercise.

When you start your presentation with an audience involvement technique, audience engagement goes high, maybe not to 100 percent, but pretty high. If you do one audience technique in the beginning, one in the middle, and one at the end, this boosts overall engagement quite a lot. You need that engagement to get your content back and forth. So all this stuff is not just about being clever or confident in front of the group, or showing off. It's about math. These techniques help you get a lot more done in less time.

Sometimes, people ask me if the audience gets tired of the techniques. People who have gone through the Own the Room training, and know how the techniques work, are especially concerned about this. If you do an audience technique every minute for an hour, yes, it will wear out the audience. But if you do one every 10 to 15 minutes, it will feel fresh because you will apply the techniques a different way each time. It's like getting Novocain or an anesthetic. Even when you know it's coming, it still works. The smarter your audience is, the more they will want to show you how smart they are, the more they will want to participate. Life is not a spectator sport. People want to play.

I have seen this over and over. People get the idea behind the techniques and practice them, but that only gets them halfway across the bridge. The first time you apply them in real life, it does feel weird. But, it comes to feel natural very quickly. Go boldly across the bridge. The other side feels terrific.

SUMMARY

★ Involving your audience members in your presentation prevents them from becoming distracted and lets them know that they are important to you.

★ Audience involvement techniques can provide you with important data about who the people in your audience are and how they feel about your topic. Do something with the data.

★ A technique such as a pair-up gives you, the speaker, a break.

★ You can use audience involvement techniques to open and close your talk, as well as throughout the presentation.

★ Plan out your audience involvement techniques. You don't want to stop during your presentation to think of a creative body poll.

Practice

The best people to practice on are the innocent people in your private life. The next time you are trying to make a decision with your family or friends, think of the most creative body poll you can to reach a consensus. Are you trying to decide what type of food to order, what movie to see, or where to go on vacation? Have people act out their choice and move toward the people with the same choice. If you experiment in fun situations—on the waiter, someone on public transportation, or a coworker in an elevator—using the techniques during a business presentation will become easier.

CHAPTER 15

———

Easy Openings
You Can Imagine

★

*There are three things to aim at in public speaking: first, to get
into your subject, then to get your subject into yourself, and,
lastly, to get your subject into the heart of your audience.*
—ALEXANDER GREGG

Imagine the most beautiful place on the planet that you have ever vis-
ited, the most beautiful place in the whole world where you personally
have ever been. Imagine you are there right now. What sounds do you
hear around you? What are the smells? Take a deep breath. How does
it feel to be there?

Remember the classic television shows *Gilligan's Island*, *The
Brady Bunch*, and *Cheers*? How did all those shows start? With a signature theme song. These songs were popular. *Cheers* was rated the
the number one theme song of all time. *Gilligan's Island* was rated
number six, and *The Brady Bunch* was number ten.

Now think about the top television shows today. My wife, Maria's,
favorite shows are *CSI* and *NCIS*. How do these shows begin?

It doesn't matter what the series or episode is. It starts with a dead
body in a parking lot in Vegas. *Then* comes the theme song.

Why the switch? Why did the television industry change how it
opens?

I did not know the answer—I am not that bright—but we were
working with people in the industry. One at CBS joked, "We should

call ourselves the crime channel and be done with it," and I asked him, "Why the switch?" I assumed that it was about grabbing people's attention quickly and drawing them into the program. That part was true, but the real reason for the change? Money! Go figure. An industry that wanted to make more money. Who would have guessed?!

Producers realized that even when viewers loved a show so much that they planned their whole week around it, they didn't tune in during the theme song. When the theme song comes on, they could walk to the fridge to get a sandwich because they knew that they weren't missing anything important. They could skip the commercial break that followed the theme song and be back in front of the television in time for the start of the show.

But if *CSI* is your favorite show, do you want to miss the first 30 seconds? No, because those 30 seconds are critical to the story. Running that 30-second scene before the opening credits, and then the theme song, ensures that viewers will already have their sandwich and be sitting there when the commercials come on. If more eyeballs are watching the commercials, then the network can charge advertisers more.

Okay, but what does this have to do with your presenting? I don't know. I just think it's interesting.

Oh wait, there is a point. When you are speaking before an audience, you want to give people the dead body, not the theme song. When you start your presentation with a predictable opening, such as, "Hi, my name is . . . ," "Thank you so much for . . . ," "We are here today to talk about . . . ," you are giving your audience members your personal theme song. And where will they go mentally when you do this? Right, they'll go get that sandwich.

The beginning of most presentations and meetings, unfortunately, follows this formulaic approach of the speaker introducing herself, thanking the host, and then telling the audience what she is going to talk about during her presentation. It sounds polite and reasonable, but openings of this type are also quite ineffective, and they unintentionally raise the audience's filters. All audiences prejudge, and if the first 30 seconds offer nothing new, what will an audience think the rest of the session is going to be like?

However, if the first 30 seconds of your presentation offer something different or unusual, filters will go down. Opening with a story or a scene accomplishes this.

The shortest presidential inaugural speech was given
by George Washington in 1789. It was 135 words
long. William Henry Harrison gave the longest
inaugural speech, with 8,445 words.
He died the next month of pneumonia from being
exposed to the cold and wet during his speech.

Michael: Okay, I get the part about lowering filters, but don't I *have* to say hi and that I'm glad to be here and thank the person who introduced me?

Coach: As for what you *have* to do, that is up to you. I like the line from *Dances with Wolves* where Kevin Costner's character asks Ten Bears what he should do. Ten Bears has the best answer: "No man can tell another man what to do." So you decide what you *want* to do. But you should know that "Hi, I'm glad to be here. My name is Michael. Here is what I am going to talk about" is your theme song. It's what is expected, and it is making filters go up, not down.

I have done a lot of seminars, and I haven't introduced myself in years. Even if people don't already know who I am, they will get to know me a little during the session, and I will get to know them.

Michael: But isn't it rude not to say thank you and introduce yourself?

Coach: Who matters, you or the audience?

Michael: The audience, of course.

Coach: So whom do most speakers introduce first?

Michael: Themselves.

Coach: Why?

continued

> **Michael:** I guess because they feel it is expected. And maybe also because they feel a need to give their credentials. Maybe it is because they are nervous or insecure?
>
> **Coach:** Of course, and that's all completely natural and normal. I was no different. But rise to the next level and make it about the audience *first*. Involve people *first*. The more you are interested in them, the more they will be interested in you. Then when you do tell them about yourself, do it in a way that is relevant, timely, different, and fitting to the situation.

Your primary task at the beginning of your presentation is to lower the audience's filters and get people thinking about your topic. Everything hinges on those two components. We are attached to the boring, formulaic opening because we've seen it so many times. We think it is expected, but let it go. The people in your audience will tune you out. They will know it's just an introduction and not important.

Consider this opening:

> Hi, everyone, and thanks, Professor, for the introduction. I'm Miguel Sanchez and I am a student here at the university. I'm really glad to be here today to talk about our class project. It's a topic we have a lot of passion for. . . .

This is a normal, standard opening, so let's analyze it.

Most of us, when we are in front of a new audience, will feel a strong need to establish our credibility and our credentials. Much of this stems from natural and well-meaning tendencies. We are anticipating and answering the questions our audience may have about us. But part of this is also motivated by our insecurity, and because we are copying older habits of other people.

Let go of the need to establish your credibility up front. If it is necessary, slip some in early but not first. If you focus on the people in your audience first—on engaging them, involving them, and establishing a strong connection with them—your credibility will establish itself.

Easy Openings

You may be thinking, "Okay, Bill, I can't open with my usual 'theme song.' So, how do I open?" Can you think of any technique we've learned so far in this book that might work as an opening?

Imagine: Setting a Scene

Let's say, for example, that you are standing before an audience, about to give a presentation about a charity for which you are trying to raise support—an organization that helps poor women and children in an impoverished third-world country. You could say, "Hi, my name is ___, and I am the executive director of ABC. I am here today to raise money to provide sanitary medical care for women and their babies in XYZ. . . ."

Or, the first words out of your mouth could be:

> Imagine that you are a young mother who is about to give birth. You live in a hut with a dirt floor and no running water, electricity, or indoor plumbing. You are feeling contractions, and you know that the hospital is a two-day walk away. You thought the baby wasn't coming for two more weeks, but now you know it will only be a few hours. Imagine the dust and heat and humidity, the flies and mosquitoes. Imagine the physical pain as you deliver your baby on that dirt floor, the pain in your heart as you worry about your baby's survival. . . ."

Okay, that was a very dramatic example of using the word *imagine* to set a scene, but you *got the picture*.

Now it's your turn. Imagine that you are the sales representative for a vacation resort. A tropical island, a family amusement park, a Rocky Mountain ski lodge—it's your choice. Now, using the word *imagine* to start your pitch—and you can repeat the word *imagine* as many times as you need to throughout the presentation—set the scene for your potential customers. Use strong and vivid language to transport them onto your tropical island, or to send them swooshing down the slopes.

But first, get out your video camera and prepare to record yourself.

Ready? You have one minute to set your scene. Record yourself, then play back, then delete.

BEGIN.

There are many approaches for using the imagine technique.

Time

> Past (Imagine you are 5 years old about to go off to school for the first time.)

> Present (Imagine the competition is on the other side of town meeting and talking about us right now. What are they saying?)

> Future (Imagine you retired 10 years ago and you are sitting at your kitchen table, looking at your bank statements.)

Asking your audience to recall or imagine a place in time then gives you the opportunity to ask a few people to share the scene they've conjured up. This allows you not only to involve the audience members and keep their filters lowered, but to get to know them and how they think and feel.

Outliers/Extremes

Ask the audience:

> What was the best . . . ?

> What was the worst . . . ?

> Why?

With this opening, you can either go around the room or ask a few members of the audience to share their best or worst memory or experience on the subject. As in the time example, this will allow you to involve the audience members and get to know them. Their best and worst experiences or memories of a topic related to your presentation provide you with very valuable and useful information.

Get your video camera ready and prepare an imagine opening using the time or the outlier approach. Record, play back, and delete.

Ready?

BEGIN.

Tell a Story

What if, using the same set of facts, instead of setting just a scene, we told a story? If you're doing sales for a vacation resort, you've probably spent some wonderful times there yourself. Maybe you helped a couple plan their perfect anniversary getaway. Or, if we were to return to the example of our third-world charity, we might start with:

> Mary was a young woman living in XYZ who was expecting her first child. She lived in a dirt-floor hut that was a two-day walk from the nearest hospital. . . .

Again, you get the picture.

Now, set up your video camera again and record yourself making a one-minute pitch, but this time, open with a story. Remember, record, play back, then delete.

Ready?

BEGIN.

Setting scenes and telling stories are extremely powerful tools for public speaking and giving presentations, but for your purposes as a speaker, they are especially powerful in the opening. Stories and scenes pull your audience right into your presentation and establish an immediate connection. You will have evoked the emotion you want to evoke right from the start.

Of course, if you are going to open with a story, you want it to be a good story, and you want to tell it well. First and foremost, the story you choose to tell or the scene you decide to set should relate directly to the topic of your presentation and evoke the emotion that you want your audience to feel. You also want it to be brief and to the point.

Remember, this is just the opening of your presentation, a technique to lower filters, connect with those in your audience, and signal to them that you are going to be an interesting and dynamic speaker. You still have to get through your content.

Can we think of some other techniques for easy openings?

Open with a Statistic

"Did you know that 10,000 mothers and babies die in childbirth each year in the country of XYZ?"

Open with a Body Poll

"Show me with your . . ." I start probably half of my real-life speeches with a body poll. It instantly involves the audience members, gets the cell phones put away, and lets me direct them in a line of thinking that fits the topic.

Open with a Question

"How many women and babies do you think die during childbirth each year in the country of XYZ?"

Statistics, body polls, and questions are all powerful opening techniques that will enable you to engage your audience, establish a connection, and evoke an emotional response.

Okay, you know the drill. Get your camera rolling, and record yourself opening first with a statistic (you can make one up for the purpose of practicing), then with a body poll, and then with a question. Record, play back, and delete.

Ready?

BEGIN.

Don't Be Afraid to Be Different

Despite the power and effectiveness of these opening techniques, many executives I have trained are particularly resistant to abandoning the old standard—and ineffective—opening format. One of the strongest areas of resistance I get from students during this aspect of training concerns thanking the host. Is it important to thank your host? Absolutely. It is absolutely important. Let's take a moment, however, to tap into our creativity and think of different ways we can thank our host without reverting to the same old theme song.

Could we give our host a compliment that highlights a standout accomplishment or skill?

Could we tell a brief story about our host that makes him look good?

Could we present her with a little gift or tribute?

If you can find different and unusual ways to thank your host, you will accomplish two goals at the same time: you will make your host feel special while also lowering your audience members' filters.

I once worked with a famous football coach, now on the speaking circuit, to devise a thank you to the host that was perfect for him. Here is what we created:

Early in his speech, he would take a new football out of the box. He would talk about the power of teams as he held up the football, tossing it back and forth with members of the audience. This interaction created energy in the room and kept the audience members engaged and their filters low, because they didn't know if the football would be tossed to them next. Toward the end, he would pull out a special marker and ask everyone in the audience to sign the football as he tossed it around the room.

At the end of his speech, he would call the host who was responsible for inviting him (and, let's not forget, paying him) to the stage and say, "There is a tradition that all champions practice. They present a game ball to the MVP. Let's all thank our MVP, who made today possible."

Then he'd hand the host the signed football.

The football coach realized that thanking the host at the beginning of his speech would have been nice, but quickly forgotten. Thanking the host at the end of the presentation by giving him or her the "game ball" on stage—usually with a fantastic photo op—became a priceless memory for the host. You can bet that the ball was placed prominently on an office shelf or in a display case afterward, triggering stories and conversations going forward.

SUMMARY

★ Let go of the need to introduce yourself and establish your credibility up front. If you focus on engaging, involving, and establishing a strong connection with your audience, your credibility will establish itself.

★ You have two jobs as a presenter: to lower your audience members' filters and to orient them in the direction you want them to go. The success of your presentation depends on achieving those two objectives.

★ Forget the "theme song" and open with a scene: a story, statistic, quote, or question that pulls your audience into the *middle* of the scene.

Practice

Find a coworker, colleague, family member, or friend to be your partner. Set a timer for 60 seconds. Choose a scene to set for your partner: perhaps your favorite vacation spot or a crisis at work. Each sentence *must* begin with the word *imagine*. Continue doing this until time runs out.

Now, ask your partner to rate, on a scale from one to ten, how well you evoked the scene.

Try it again. This time, instead of using the word *imagine*, set the scene using words, but no sentences—for example, "lake . . . summer . . . girl . . ."

Try this exercise as a group activity with your staff. Pair up people and have them take turns setting scenes for each other in 60-second intervals, using the word *imagine* to start each new sentence.

CHAPTER 16

Close with Commitment

*Leadership: the art of getting someone else to do
something you want done because they want to do it.*
—Dwight D. Eisenhower

You finish a rocking speech on physical fitness. How would you close?

You wrap up a very productive meeting on how we can all, in our work space, be more green and environmentally proactive (save money and save the planet). How do you finish that meeting?

What do great movies, books, concerts, and shows all have in common? They have a great ending. It fulfills the audience members in such a satisfying way that the experience stays with them long after they've left the theater or stadium, or turned the final page of the novel. We've all had these experiences. Maybe you've been so unnerved by a scary movie that you can't sleep for a few nights, or you find yourself glancing over your shoulder when you're walking down the street. Maybe you find yourself humming or singing a show tune or a song that you just can't get out of your head.

As a speaker, you want your presentation to stay with the people in your audience long after they leave the room. Being memorable is important, but it's only the beginning—a means, but not an end.

I will often ask a student, "What did you want your audience to do?" As Michael Balaoing says, "WTF." What's the *feeling* you want everyone to have?

People often look befuddled (apparently, a common effect I have on people) and say, "Well, I just wanted them to know X or understand Y."

That is not enough. If your goal is just to have people understand your topic, then often, your message will be like water through their fingers. They do understand, for a minute, but they won't remember. You have to give your audience a vessel to "hold" that understanding. That vessel is an action. When you get your audience to *act*, the understanding comes along for the ride. When you focus only on what you want people to *know*, action rarely leaves the parking lot.

You want your audience to *do* something—to buy your product, to contribute to your fund-raiser, to meet the new sales goals you've just outlined. The closing of your presentation must prompt the people in your audience to action. That's why you were speaking before them in the first place; that's the point of your presentation. Your goal is not to convince your audience that your nonprofit group does great work. Your goal is to get people to write a check. One of my college roommates had a cruder version of this philosophy: "How the date ends, dude, is how the date went."

In the first chapter of this book, I asked you to pour some water into your hands and try to hold onto it. The water slipped through your fingers because you did not have a container to hold it in. The exercise was intended to pull you into *attack* mode, to get you actively engaged in the process of learning. During our in-person trainings, I revive that technique to demonstrate a second, different message.

Most speakers have a wonderful message; they succeed in motivating their audience and inspiring strong feelings and emotions in their audience, but they don't give the audience anything in which it can hold the message and the emotions. The audience members can feel the message and the emotions wash over them, but within moments of the presentation being over, they are bombarded by competing messages, both externally and internally, and by the time they walk out the door, the message and the feelings have dissipated.

Great leaders ask questions that lead the individual to
solve the problem or create the opportunity . . .
hence learning takes place.
—DAVID BALL

As speakers, we need to give the people in our audience a vessel or container in which they can hold our message. That vessel is action. When we close our presentations by prompting the audience members to act, they will hold our message in their memory permanently. If the audience members don't commit to an action, the message and emotions you have given them will slip through their fingers.

For example, let's say you just gave a presentation on how to reduce supply costs in your office. An effective closing thought would be to ask everyone in the room to commit to one idea of her own choosing to help the company slash waste.

> We talked about what we, as a group, will do to reduce the cost and waste of supplies, but let's close with everyone making a commitment. I am going to go around the room, and I want everyone to answer this question: What are you personally going to do toward this effort?

What did we just do? We just used the audience involvement technique of going around the room to prompt our audience to action. You can use a number of audience involvement techniques—body poll, pair up, survey, or, in this case, closing thought—to answer the action question. The key is that the action you are asking for meets the following criteria:

1. Simple enough for people to realistically commit

2. A step in the right direction

It doesn't have to be a big step. A baby step in the right direction that everyone takes is better than a giant step that no one takes.

During one training session I conducted, a participant gave a presentation on the dangers of texting while driving. At the end of the class, he asked everyone to commit to never texting while driving. The audience members sort of agreed and nodded their heads. Afterward, we asked the audience members to raise their hands if they really thought they would never text while driving again. No one raised a hand. The audience members told us that they agreed in order to be polite, but they did not think that they could realistically promise never to text while driving. One person said that he agreed with the message and the principle, but he probably would not stick to the pledge.

The speaker then adjusted his approach, asking the audience to commit to absolutely not texting while driving for the *rest of that day*. Everyone agreed to this, and when we polled the audience, each person said that he or she would probably stick to the promise.

Then we tried one more approach. We went around the room and asked each person to say how long he or she could commit to not texting while driving, but first we asked people to really think about it, and not to say anything that they didn't mean. We asked them to be brutally honest and give only a time frame they believed they could commit to 100 percent. If they weren't sure, or if they didn't want to do it, we gave them an escape clause. They could just say, "I want to think about it."

Whether it was one day or one week or longer, we asked the audience members to commit only to what they were sure they could deliver. We then went around the room, and each person gave an answer. Afterward, the session participants said that they thought this technique produced the biggest commitment.

Your closing action should be a small task that is simple enough for people to actually, really do it.

Let's try another example. You are promoting a brand, so you ask the members of your audience to "like" your brand on Facebook once they get home. What if, instead, you asked the audience to take out their mobile phone or device, click on Facebook, and "like" your brand right then and there? Done. Instead of asking people to do it later and hoping that they won't forget, you have turned it into a group activity that took only a few minutes.

Maybe you are giving a speech to promote an organization that helps military veterans. You could ask your audience members to send a card to a veteran, thanking her for her service. Maybe they will go home and do it. Or, you can ask them to reach under their chairs, where you have placed a thank you card and a pen. Ask them to write the card right then and there, on the spot. Do you think they will be more likely to pop it into the mail? *The point is to figure out a way to have your audience members do something right then, in the room, that will lead them to do something more later.*

In our training sessions, one of the ways we teach this technique is to hand out cards with topics printed on them. We then ask each participant to come up with some simple, directional tasks to ask an audience to do based on the topic he or she has drawn. When you are preparing for your presentations, you want to prepare a closing that will include an action request.

Whichever technique you decide to use to secure a closing action, you must also let the people in your audience know that they will be accountable for seeing their commitment through. Be clear on the deadline by which they are expected to take that action, and the means through which they are expected to report back to you.

Cook Up Something with Your Family

Parade magazine reaches tens of millions of readers every Sunday through hundreds of newspapers. I've had the pleasure of working with the wonderful publisher, Jack Haire, and editor in chief, Maggie Murphy, on a range of projects.

One day, *Parade* asked me to work with one of its star talents, Jon Ashton, the celebrity chef from Britain. Jon was embarking on a cross-country tour, starting in Pittsburgh. A couple of thousand people had paid money to watch Jon cook on stage for a couple of hours, and if you met him, you would understand why. Entertaining, charming, and genuine, Jon doesn't "fancy himself a celebrity chef."

Jon didn't need much help or coaching, but when we got to the end, we talked about what could make a great closing. I asked what he normally did for a closing, and what his goal was for his cooking demonstrations.

One of his themes is getting families to cook together, so we devised the following closing for him:

> The last two minutes are the most important of the two hours, because now you are the celebrity chef in your own kitchen. I want everyone to pick a partner and turn and face me.
>
> Now, when I say, "Go," I want you all to make a commitment. We are all in this together. You are going to commit to your partner that you are going to make a meal together with your family within the next week. What day, and what theme. That's it. The rest you can decide later. Pick which day and what theme. For example, you could say, "I am going to do Mexican for Tuesday breakfast, or Italian on Friday for dinner." But don't say it unless you are really going to do it. You have 30 seconds. Ready? Go!
>
> Okay, turning back this way, raise your hands if you made a commitment. When they bring a microphone to you, say it nice and loud when I point to you.

Jon then had a few people share their meal commitment, which built more energy in the room. He told them which website to go to after the family meal to tell him and all of us how it went.

If Jon had not done all that at the closing, how many people would have cooked a meal with their families in the next week? A few, for sure. But when he did a closing with a call to action and commitment, how many more do you think did it? I don't know either, but I'm willing to bet that the number is higher.

Your presentation is your gift to your audience. The call to action is what makes the gift last longer.

Whichever technique you decide to use to secure a closing action, you must let your audience members know that they will be accountable for seeing their commitment through. Be clear on the deadline by which they are expected to take that action, and on the means through which they can share or report back.

SUMMARY

★ Close your presentation by asking the people in your audience to commit to an action.

★ The key to persuading people lies in what you ask them to do. Ask yourself, what do you want the audience members to do, and what questions will offer them a chance to act?

★ The closing action should be simple and easy, something that your audience can do immediately.

★ Create a follow-up mechanism. Make sure your audience members know that they will be accountable for completing that action.

Practice

You are making a speech to a large audience on the third floor of a conference center. The topic is health and physical fitness. You are amazing. Well, of course you are. Informative. Inspirational. But now that it's time for the close, what could you do? Film yourself trying different closings.

CHAPTER 17

Leveraging Team Presentations

★

Getting the players is easy.
Getting them to play together is the hard part.
—CASEY STENGEL

Thirty years ago, how many news anchors usually delivered the news? Write your answer here: ____

Now, in any city in the world *today*, on any television station, when you turn on the news, how many people are delivering the news? Write your answer here: ____

Why did the industry change? Why did it go from one anchor to a team?

Write your opinion here: _____

_____

One of the key people collaborating on this book, Robin Wallace, who also writes for one of the cable news networks, understands better than I do what news producers figured out a while ago: having multiple people cohost the program broadened the audience appeal of the broadcast. A viewer who didn't care for one anchor might tune in because he liked the other; the coanchors and the other members of the on-air team interact with one another on camera, infusing the broadcast with energy and entertainment, and creating a much more dynamic newscast.

Today, the evening news is delivered by an entire team. It doesn't matter what station you watch. There are a man and a woman, maybe a wacky weather person, and a sports personality.

Team presentations are a growing trend in your sector, too. When done well, the team approach can be extremely effective and can achieve better results than a one-person show. Teams create energy, bring some entertainment to the proceedings, and keep filters down. Team presentations and audience involvement are growing trends because audiences respond to them.

Many of the techniques for individual presentations that we have learned so far can and should be employed by a team for the same reasons, and to accomplish the same objectives. From voice modulation, to audience involvement, to strong language and powerful openings, the techniques that are effective for an individual are also effective for a team. The first step in planning a team presentation is determining whether an individual or a group approach is the best strategy for the presentation.

The strength of the team is each individual member.
The strength of each member is the team.
—PHIL JACKSON

Team presentations are usually the best option when no one person has the knowledge and the expertise necessary to give the entire presentation. For example, if your company is rolling out a new software application, you may want to have someone from engineering discuss the amazing technology behind the application and how it works, and someone from marketing lay out the research and data showing which segment of the population is the best target market for the product. Then, someone from sales could go over the strategy for reaching that ideal target market. The most important factor in putting together a team presentation is to make sure that everyone on the team has a role. Not everyone on the team will necessarily be required to speak or will have an equally important role, but each should have a clear function.

Let's look at how some of our core techniques apply to team presentations.

Eliminate Weak Language

"Okay, now I am going to hand off to my colleague, Joe," or, "Thank you for the hands off, Trista."

These are examples of weak language, team versions of the individual "Today I am going to talk about . . ." theme song opening that we want to avoid. Team presentations need strong transitions, which can be achieved using any of the techniques we have learned so far. It is not necessary to formally introduce your colleague, or to tell the audience that you are about to "hand off." Close your part of the presentation strongly, with an action closing, just as you would if you were a solo presenter. The team member who follows you should be prepared with her own strong opening.

Be Creative

Team presentations allow you to expand upon your creativity exponentially. For example, you can position the members of your team at different points in the room, pass around props, act out demonstrations, and role-play. One of the best ways to grow people in sales, or in almost any area, is to engage them in simple role-playing exercises in which they are able to view a situation from different perspectives and improve how they handle both opportunities and challenges. The possibilities are endless.

Chemistry Matters

Let's tune in to our favorite news program. Is it NBC or FOX? CNN or MSNBC? Each of these news outlets has its own distinctive, signature style, and we could discuss these differences at length. But they all have something very much in common as well: the chemistry among the members of their news teams. We see team members listening attentively to one another's reports, laughing together, commending and thanking one another for a job well done. They appear to be one big, happy family, and our mirror neurons respond to that chemistry. We feel like we're part of the family as well.

We have all seen programs and presentations in which team members or panels seem to be in conflict with one another, or where the chemistry is off or wrong. The audience will mirror that tension and awkwardness, and become alienated by the bad chemistry. The lesson: support your teammates during group presentations.

Recognize the Audience as a Member of Your Team

When a team has worked together to create a group presentation, its members can often get so caught up in what they have decided to cover that they forget about their audience. The presentation becomes more about the team, and not enough about the audience. The audience cares about its own agenda, not yours. All of the same rules for lowering filters, connecting with your audience, getting over yourself, and remembering that it's all about the audience apply to team presentations.

There are no more individual presentations for you guys. For the rest of your life, think of every presentation as a team presentation. Even if it's just you on stage in front of a thousand people. All of those people are on your team if you start to imagine them that way.

Body Language

Let's say that you are giving your part of a team presentation. While you are speaking, one of your team members standing behind you is looking at his watch, shifting his weight from one foot to the other, and glancing out the window or up at the ceiling. His body language is undermining what you are saying to the audience. Because body language is such a powerful element of communication, we are always sending messages with our gestures, movements, and facial expressions.

During training sessions, when we videotape students practicing a given technique, the tapes of the team training sessions usually catch people drifting off while another member of their team is speaking. What would happen if, during a team presentation, all three members of your team began to speak at the same time, with each person telling the audience something entirely different? This is exactly what happens when one person is communicating with the audience with words and the other members of the team are communicating through body language. Everyone is speaking to the audience at the same time. If the audience is getting a cacophony of messages, it will raise its filters against the noise.

Your body language should strengthen your colleague's message. When a member of your team is speaking, you should be looking directly at him, sending him positive energy.

During our in-person coaching sessions, the video never lies:

Coach: What do you see here in the video, where Alessandra is speaking and the other four are standing? How are they standing? Let's rewind and watch it again.

Andy: One of them is watching her; two are looking away.

Margo: And one is completely distracted.

continued

Coach: How many people on the team are communicating at once?

Stuart: All of them.

Coach: Very good. Because body language is such a large part of communicating, we are always sending messages. I have had the chance to get to know a few politicians from across the spectrum, from Governor Jeb Bush in Florida to Senator Harris Wofford in Pennsylvania, and, of course, I love all politicians equally. (*smiling*) I am often asked, "Who are the best speakers?" There are some excellent speakers in politics; Ronald Reagan and Bill Clinton come to mind. President Obama, certainly. I never met Hillary Clinton, but during her run for president, I noticed that often Bill (President Clinton, sorry; it's not like I am friends with him) was on stage. What did he have to do during her whole speech?

Angelika: Look at her.

Coach: And how did he have to look at her?

Roman: Adoringly. (*everyone laughs*)

Coach: Exactly. He had to look at her like "that was the most intelligent thing I have ever heard a human being say" for 40 minutes. If he had looked at his watch once while she was speaking, "click"—that could have been on CNN.

Through his body language, President Clinton strengthened and supported her message, letting the audience members know that it was worthy of their undivided attention. Had he seemed distracted, the world would have gotten a very different message.

When you are part of a team presentation, you have several options when your colleagues are speaking:

> You can face them and give them support with your body language.

> You can study the room and read the audience, assessing who is engaged and thinking up options to engage the others.

You can echo what your colleague is saying to the audience by writing key points on a whiteboard or flipchart while she is speaking. (Make sure the speaker finds this helpful first.)

You can set up for the next piece in the presentation, but be sure you do not create a distraction by doing so. If you have to write out a sign or prepare a video camera, do it in the back of the room or offstage.

Identify One Person to Take Charge

Choose one team member to play the role of stage manager. This person will keep the presentation running smoothly and be empowered to make decisions on the spot, if that becomes necessary. You do not want your team holding a debate before your audience (unless that was part of the plan). When a matter must be decided instantly, defer to the person in charge. He can pass the decision back to others as needed.

Build on One Another's Strengths

Successful team presentations require chemistry among the team members, firmness on the goal of the presentation, and flexibility on the strategy for reaching that goal. If the team members are not "clicking" with one another, you may want to reconsider the plan. Team members should complement one another in terms of personality, knowledge, and talent.

Firmness in goal, but flexibility of strategy, is a key concept that we teach in our executive training and management courses—and one that we will examine in depth in a later chapter in this book on managing meetings—but it also applies to public speaking when the presentation involves a team approach. The goal of the presentation must be firm. Are you introducing a new product? Outlining a problem with a client? You must know what your goal is and what you want to accomplish, and be firm on this point.

How to achieve that goal—the strategy—requires flexibility. Perhaps one team member thinks the group should act out a commercial, while another favors a more traditional approach. One may want to open with a body poll, while another wants to stun the audience with a startling statistic. These are all strategies for the presentation, and team members should be open to one another's ideas. This is where teams need flexibility.

Let the spotlight shine, in some capacity, on all the team members. It will give each of them more credit and credibility, which will resonate with the audience. Audience members will be impressed with the fact that your company or organization has a deep bench of talent and expertise working on the job.

Don't Overplan Before Your First Dry Run

When you are planning your presentations, instead of spending an hour planning, then doing a quick run-through before you go live, spend a half hour planning and more time practicing. During these dry runs, be open to the fact that your presentation won't be perfect, and allow yourself to laugh at your mistakes. Then, do more planning and more practice. The purpose of the practice run is not just to determine the length of the presentation; it's a time to identify weaknesses and make necessary modifications. Ask one another, "Did that sound boring? Did we involve the audience at all? If we were the audience, what would we be feeling? How do we reach those extra three centimeters?"

You want to practice, refine, modify, and polish, but you do not want to become overly attached to your plan. In the history of all team presentations, not one has yet gone completely according to plan, and that's okay. Your audience does not know what your plan was, or what was *supposed* to happen, so it won't know that something is going wrong. However, if you become flustered or upset or thrown off because the presentation is not going as planned, your audience *will* pick up on that.

SUMMARY

★ Team presentations are usually the best option when no one person has the knowledge and expertise necessary for the entire presentation.

★ Group presentations can make for more dynamic, entertaining, and creative presentations.

★ Teams can often get so caught up in their presentations that they forget about the audience. All of the rules about focusing on your audience still apply.

★ The audience involvement techniques that are effective in individual presentations are equally effective in team presentations.

★ Spend less time planning and more time practicing.

Practice

For your next presentation, try the team approach. Recruit some of your colleagues to play a role or to contribute their expertise. Junior colleagues are likely to jump at the chance to participate in a team presentation with you.

PART IV

THE
WHOLE WORLD
IS A STAGE

There are many ways in which we can apply these star presenting skills in different formats:

★ One-on-one conversations

★ Meetings and conference calls

★ Panels

★ Keynotes

★ Sales pitches

CHAPTER 18

One-on-One Conversations: Use Active Listening to Get People to Hang on Your Every Word

The fool wonders. The wise man asks.
—Benjamin Disraeli

Imagine that you are the leader of a dynamic and innovative organization, and that you have a talented and aggressive sales team reporting to you. Diane has been a member of your sales team for five years, and she is a solid performer. She's not a superstar, but you can count on her to produce, to meet goals and expectations, and to approach her work with enthusiasm.

Lately, however, the Diane you've come to depend on seems to be out to lunch—both literally and figuratively. She's been coming in late and ducking out early, and she seems distracted at meetings. She's showing up and clocking in—nothing is dramatically wrong—but the quality of her work has not been up to her usual standard. You summon Diane for a meeting to discuss her job performance. Sitting behind your desk, you review your concerns.

"Diane, I was looking for you yesterday, and you'd left early. I'm concerned about the Jones account. You don't seem to be on top of things," you say.

Diane is nervous, uncomfortable, and possibly embarrassed. Maybe she's a little defensive. How does Diane respond to your review of her job performance?

She says, "I'm sorry. I promise I'll do better," or something to that effect. Maybe she offers some type of weak explanation. You dismiss her, and she shuffles back to her desk. Nothing changes.

Now let's hit rewind and rewrite the script for that meeting.

Diane enters your office, and you invite her to take a seat. You turn away from you computer, slide the papers on your desk to one side, and lean across your desk toward her:

> **You:** Diane, I wanted to follow up with you on the Jones account. What's behind this delay?
>
> **Diane:** Bob has had to cancel several scheduled calls, but he's assured me that he's available for our call this afternoon.
>
> **You:** This afternoon. Great! I actually wanted to touch base with you yesterday, but you'd already left for the day. Is everything okay?
>
> **Diane:** Well . . . just that my mother fell, and she's alone.
>
> **You:** Is she all right?
>
> **Diane:** Yes, well, she's back in the hospital, so . . .

Let's stop this meeting at this point for now.

The first example is typical of meetings and conversations of this type. It is an example of what we call *passive listening*. As an employer, you list your concerns about an employee's job performance, and then hear your employee say some version of, "I'm sorry; I will do better." But, did you extract any information from the employee that explains why his job performance has declined? Did you hear all the things the employee is *not saying*?

The second scenario is an example of *active listening*. When we *actively listen*, we ask active questions. By actively listening, you discovered that Diane's mother is ill and has been in and out of the hospital.

You learned that this situation is why she is leaving work early during crunch time on a crucial account. And if you were listening *very actively*, you may have also heard that Diane does not have the best relationship with Bob and is frustrated by it.

When you are conducting a one-on-one meeting or conversation of this nature, passive listening will get you only as far as, "I'm sorry; I will do better." That response does not provide you with any information that you can use to improve the situation. Through active listening, you "hear" that perhaps a spouse or parent is ill, or that your employee is experiencing unusual stress in her personal life. You *want* to "hear" that he is frustrated professionally, or that she feels that her work has not been appropriately recognized or appreciated. If you are actively listening, you may "hear" that this otherwise valued employee is considering a competing job offer, and is looking for you to give her a reason to stay.

In many cases, your employee is not going to volunteer this information. More likely, he will be withdrawn and doing everything he can to provide you with as little information as possible. It is your responsibility to find out what's really going on through active listening.

The greatest superpower of speakers is the ability to *read* the audience, to *listen to* and *hear* the audience, including what it *doesn't* say. The same concept applies to an audience of one. Active listening helps you connect with your audience so that you can read your audience.

Active listening takes work and uses a lot of energy. It tires you out, and you will feel a sense of depletion afterward. But just think about the advantages that the ability to read your audience accurately will provide for you. Now think about the degree to which those speakers who cannot read their audience are at a disadvantage.

Returning to our example, by actively listening to Diane, you've learned that she is going through a tough time and is distracted. As an understanding and caring and wonderful boss, you may or may not cut her some slack during this time, but your decision will be based on a decent diagnosis of the situation. However, you may also want to reassign that crucial Jones account or put some extra support staff on it.

Without the data gleaned through active listening, you would not have the information you need to make the best decision for your employee *and* your company.

Active listening is not our default setting. Although it requires many core principles of all public speaking—getting over yourself; understanding that it's not about you, it's about your audience; focusing on your audience; hearing and reading your audience—many of the situations in which we need to use active listening also involve delicate matters or conflict. We are struggling to lower our own filters because we don't want to deal with conflict or with awkward or uncomfortable situations. Instead, we wind up in passive-aggressive mode, which can be contagious. We know it is immature and unprofessional, but it's easy to get stuck there. And, we all know how pleasant and fun to deal with passive-aggressive people are. But if you coach enough people, you see that no one really *wants* to be passive-aggressive. No one wakes up in the morning thinking, how can I be a little immature today? We just get trapped, and it feels hard to step out of it.

Active listening is an advanced skill that does require some work to develop and master. However, there are several techniques that we can learn and use during our one-on-one conversations that will help us become active listeners.

Short, Open Questions

When a journalist wants information from a person, what does she do? She interviews the subject. And what happens during an interview? The journalist asks the subject questions—questions that prompt the other person to provide the information that the reporter wants.

In the first example of our meeting with Diane, you, the boss, did not ask any questions, and therefore you did not get any information. In the second example, however, you employed the technique of asking short, open questions that prompted Diane to respond with valuable information.

Some examples of short, open questions are:

Tell me more about . . .

What's behind that?

Say more . . .

Why?

And?

There are times when we need to ask longer questions, but for short, open questions, think of limiting them to five words or less. If your question is long, sometimes the question is more about you. When it's short, it can be more about the other person.

You: What's behind this delay?

Diane: Bob has had to cancel several calls . . .

Imagine that Diane's thought is a train stuck in the tunnel. She has an issue that she's reluctant to bring up, and she doesn't have enough power to push through the tunnel. She's inching out, spinning her wheels. When you ask her short, active, empathetic questions, you give her the traction to get through the tunnel and come toward you. If your question is long-winded and takes more than a sentence to ask, then Diane has to concentrate on what you are saying, and she begins to pull back the brake on her own thoughts. The entire communication has now come to a halt.

Why? Why? Why?

Those of us who have young children, or who have ever spent time with a small child, are familiar with this technique. The premise is that there is no statement and no answer to an initial question that cannot be followed up with, "Why?" For those of us who do not fall into either of these categories, or who need a refresher course, I want you for a moment to imagine a conversation—any conversation—during which, no matter what the other person says, you respond with, "Why?"

Diane: I had to leave work early yesterday.

You: Why?

Diane: My mother fell, and I was the closest one to get to her.

You: Why?

Diane: My only sibling lives four hours away . . .

In practice, you would not pepper your employee with a barrage of whys, but if you look at our example of active listening, you will see that you did ask Diane why:

You: "What's behind this delay? (*Why* haven't you closed this deal?)

In the space given here, I want you to write the answer to the following question. You can also just say it out loud, but you have to answer it.

Where do you see yourself professionally in five years? _____

_____

_____

Now, based on your answer to this question, ask yourself, "Why?"
Now, based on that answer, ask yourself again, "Why?"
Based on the previous question, ask yourself, "Why?" a third time.
How much information did you just find out about yourself that you might not have been consciously aware of? (You don't have to answer that out loud.)

Columbo's Technique

Long before there was *CSI* or *Law and Order*, there was *Columbo*, a crime show in which the great actor Peter Falk portrayed a rumpled, apparently bumbling detective who never failed to outwit and outsmart the criminals who were in his crosshairs. Columbo was a homicide detective, and the killers who thought the crazy Columbo would never catch them would find out during each episode's big climax that Columbo sure was crazy—like a fox.

Each episode ended with Columbo in a room with a guilty suspect who thought he'd gotten away with the crime. Columbo, of course, had already figured it all out, but he had a brilliant technique for tricking the bad guy into 'fessing up on his own. He would let the person talk, listening intently—and appearing to be completely confounded by what the person was saying. Columbo would then home in on just one single word the person had said, as if it contained some deep, extra meaning. With a puzzled, quizzical look on his face, he would look the suspect in the eye and repeat that one word.

> **Bad guy:** Detective, you are on the wrong track. I have a perfect alibi; there was no way I could have been there last Friday. I was nowhere near the crime scene.
>
> **Columbo:** *Last* Friday? (*quizzical look*)
>
> **Bad guy:** Yes, Friday. I told you I was not there.
>
> **Columbo:** You said *last* Friday . . . (*more puzzled look*)
>
> **Bad guy:** "Yes, I ummm . . ."
>
> **Columbo:** (*silence*)
>
> **Bad guy:** Maybe I was there on a different day, I can't remember.
>
> **Columbo:** *Different* day?

Little by little, the bad guy would start to slip up. Columbo's emphasis on the key word compelled the suspect to disclose and share more and more information.

We can use this technique. If you listen carefully to which words a person is saying seem to have a weighted meaning, simply repeating those words back to that person will direct the conversation to produce the desired information.

> **Diane:** He's had to cancel calls.
>
> **You:** *He's* canceled?
>
> **Diane:** Yes, but he says he's available today.
>
> **You:** *Today?*

Summarize

Why is it so critical for you to show the people in your audience that you are hearing them? One of the reasons is that people will often feel that they are not being heard. This, in turn, causes other problems. Once you have concluded your meeting, summarize the conversation for the person, repeating back what he has said to you. You don't want to parrot what he said, but paraphrase it, using both *his* words and *your* words. This shows the person that you have been listening to him, have heard what he has said, and have *understood* what he has said. If you have not correctly heard or understood what the person has been saying, summarizing for him will give you both the chance to clear up any miscommunication.

> **You:** Diane, being the caregiver for a sick parent can be very stressful and demanding. Do you need some personal time? Meanwhile, we've got to fix the problem with Bob.
>
> **Diane:** Yes, my mother is going to live with me while she recuperates from surgery. But, Bob is great! He's been very gracious about being unavailable, but we're on track for this afternoon.
>
> Or:
>
> **Diane:** Actually, my mother is going to go live with my sister next week, but Bob has been a little difficult. . . .

As a boss, a leader, or an employer, you cannot listen or hear everything that is going on around you or with your employees. You wouldn't have the time. However, it's your responsibility to know what you need to hear and when you must listen. You can't fix a problem if you don't know what the problem is, and you *really* can't fix it if you don't know you have a problem in the first place.

No surgeon, no matter how brilliant, would operate on a patient before first diagnosing the illness, but in business, we often treat first and diagnose second. We are too clever by half. We think we can guess what the problem or issue is, and sometimes we're right. Sometimes we are close, and sometimes we are just a little off. Sometimes, however, we are way off. Diagnose first, operate second.

Like all meetings, our one-on-one interactions with our employees have agendas and goals. You, of course, have your agenda; you are summoning an employee for a performance review or some other difficult or uncomfortable conversation. The employee also has an agenda, but she is not going to tell you what her agenda is. However, it's the employee's agenda that the meeting is going to follow. You must be able to put your agenda aside and use active listening to investigate and determine what the employee's agenda is. You will want to return to your agenda. It will be a test of your mental strength to see just how long you can stay away from your own agenda. But you cannot help your employees carry their burden if you are carrying one yourself.

As we've said, listening to your audience, hearing your audience, and reading your audience are the superpowers behind great public speaking. In one-on-one conversations, we use active listening to do this, and the techniques we use to actively listen—short and open questions, Columbo-style repeating—are audience involvement techniques for an audience of one. (They can also be used for very small groups.) And, what do our superpower hearing and audience involvement techniques accomplish for us?

They show the members of our audience that we *care about them*, which brings us full circle back to our meeting with Diane.

> **You:** Diane, you are not yourself lately. Things have been slipping, and it's not like you. (*leaning in toward her*) What's really going on? Is there something we can help you with?
>
> **Diane:** No, I'm fine. I just have some things going on, but I'm fine.
>
> **You:** C'mon. What's up?

The boss who cared enough about Diane to conduct this talk can tear up this chapter, throw it in the garbage, and stop reading. Because, guess what? If you genuinely care about your audience, you don't have to know these tips or techniques. Showing the person you're talking to that you care about him is the best technique you have. The combination of persistence and caring is powerful.

And, do you know what is the best technique for showing your audience that you care?

Actually care.

Works amazingly well. They fall for it every time.

THINK, EDIT, SPEAK

I once had a famous television actress in one of my trainings in Los Angeles. Her husband, also a relatively well-known television actor, was taking the training as well. The actress would go round and round when she spoke, and was very self-conscious about her "rambling problem."

She said she often felt like an "airhead" and asked me if I could help her.

"Can I show you something?" I asked. "Say what you just said in one sentence."

She paused for a few moments, thought about it, and then said what she'd just taken two paragraphs to say, in one sentence.

"You don't have a rambling problem; you have an editing problem."

For the actress, it was one of those watershed, breakthrough, *aha!* moments. She was thrilled with herself, and, I must say, also thrilled with me.

"You're a genius!" she cried. "You just saved me three years of therapy!"

These are the moments that, as a trainer, give me goose bumps. My friend Roberto says they're my drug. Why do I do this? It's fun. The topic is limitless, there is always so much more to learn, and every single group, every single time, makes progress. Usually the progress is incremental. But sometimes the progress is not just incremental. Sometimes it is transformative. You see someone who everyone thought was shy become bold and confident. His charisma shines through. You hear people who everyone thought were verbose become powerfully concise, and people begin to hang on their words.

This is how we came to develop a technique that we call "think, edit, speak." I suppose I have a special affinity for this technique because I used to be especially verbose and sometimes still can be. So, I appreciate even more how much people can improve. If you practice this technique 20 times, you will see yourself become powerfully concise.

Take your thumb, put it next to your temple, and say, "Think."

Take your index finger, put it over your eyeball, and say, "Edit."

Take your middle finger, put it over your mouth, and say, "Speak."

Think. Edit. Speak.

In normal life, what do *you* usually do?

You speak, edit, and think all at the same time—and you are smart enough and charming enough that you get away with it.

You know the expression "beat around the bush"? With your intelligence, you don't beat around the bush; you sprint around the bush.

But you don't have to.

Let's do a couple of repetitions. I will ask you a question, you will answer using the same rules, and you will see something start to happen in your mind. This time, show with your thumb and fingers what stage you are on.

When you leave this earth, hopefully far in the future, how do you want to be remembered?

1. Think: Thumb at your temple, as long as you want.

2. Edit: Index finger over your eyeball, as long as you want.

3. Speak: Say the brilliant sentence.

Let's do another one.

What are the most important things a boss can do to manage people well?

1. Think: Thumb at your temple, as long as you want.

2. Edit: Index finger over your eyeball, as long as you want.

3. Speak: Say the brilliant sentence.

Even though these are extremely difficult questions to answer comprehensively, do you notice anything happening in your mind?

continued

With each repetition, it is getting easier and easier for you to rein in your thoughts. Your tremendous brain speed, which was capable of beating around the bush, is now being applied to the thinking and editing phases, so you are much more articulate and impressive.

The length of the silence—the time you need to organize your thoughts—will decrease with practice, but you don't want it to shrink to less than four or five seconds. It's called being thoughtful.

In real life, even as you master "think, edit, speak," you won't use the technique all the time. Sometimes it's fun to just riff and think out loud with friends. But you will be able to do it when it is called for. You will be in a meeting, and people will turn to you and ask, "What do you think we should do?"

You will pause, consider, and give a great answer.

Here are some practice questions, but, as ever, the best people to practice on are the innocent people in your private life. When you get home, if you hear . . .

Honey, how was your day?

Say, "Hold on," and put your thumb against your temple. . . . If she thinks you are having a breakdown, maybe it will get you a free nap before dinner.

SUMMARY

★ The ability to read your audience is critical in one-on-one situations. Active listening helps you connect so that you can read your audience.

★ You cannot fix a problem until you know what the problem is. Don't guess, diagnose. And diagnose *before* you operate.

★ Think, edit, speak—in that order. Give yourself time to think about what you want to say and compose it thoughtfully before speaking.

CHAPTER 19

───

Map Out Meetings and Conference Calls

★

Never tell people how to do things.
Tell them what to do and
they will surprise you with their ingenuity.
—GEORGE PATTON

The One Big Thing to Improve Meetings: A Red Box on a Mountain

Sample meeting 1:

You have called six members of your team into a meeting to plan a staff retreat. You have allotted an hour for the meeting, and you spend that time discussing the goals of the retreat, who is coming, where it should be held, ideas for themes, and possible dates. At the end of the hour, you have not reached decisions on all of those matters, so you schedule another meeting.

Sample meeting 2:

On a flipchart behind you, you draw four red boxes. You label those boxes:

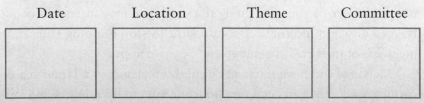

Date	Location	Theme	Committee

You then say to the staff members you've convened for the meeting:

> We have to make four decisions today; that is our goal. We will write what we decide inside these boxes, and all of us should be okay with the decisions. We have to pick the dates of the retreat, the location, what the theme will be, and who will be on the committee to then go plan all the details. Once we have achieved the goal of the meeting and filled in the four boxes, the meeting is over. We've allotted 60 minutes, but the meeting is over once we fill in these boxes.

Meeting 1 took the full hour and may or may not have reached the needed decisions. How long do you think the meeting would run in the second example?

It won't be two minutes, because everyone needs to feel good about the decisions, and these decisions will require discussion. It also won't be an hour, typically, because the members of the group (all of whom are alligators and busy people) have an incentive to reach the goal of the meeting. If the facilitator, or anyone else, gets off track, the other attendees will help pull the meeting back on track. In this meeting, people are still able to offer their opinions, but because they are focused, the meeting will probably take closer to a half hour. The facilitator and the group can then use a variety of different processes to make the decisions.

I've shared with you some pretty dismal statistics about the productivity and efficiency of meetings. You knew it all already. Meetings can be effective, but often they are not efficient. There's a big difference.

Do you want to shave a half hour off your workday? Do you want to spend more of your day doing the work you love instead of being bogged down in meetings? Do you want to stop draining your staff members of their creative energy and positive morale?

Meetings can have moments of high efficiency in a larger sea of inefficiencies. You can cut a one-hour meeting to 45 minutes and still leave time for creativity (and goofing around), but first, we have to do away with some of our entrenched ideas about meetings.

After all, who taught you how to run a meeting? Did you go to meeting school? Whom did you learn from?

We learned how to run meetings from our bosses, colleagues, and peers. And whom did they learn from? Their bosses, colleagues, and peers. This inherited system of how to conduct meetings has been passed down over the years.

And what is this system?

We make a list of items to talk about—we call it an agenda—and we discuss those items until time runs out.

Why are meetings an hour long?

The length of a meeting is arbitrary. You have to pick some length of time, and it's easier to do what others do. The best way to improve the efficiency of a meeting is to determine whether the meeting is even necessary. Sometimes we meet with our staffs weekly when we could probably meet once every two weeks.

Think about the agenda for the last meeting you attended. It probably listed the subjects to be discussed in the order in which they were to be addressed. Was a goal among the items on the agenda? At any point during the meeting, did anyone express a clear goal or a desired result that the meeting was intended to produce?

According to a global Microsoft Office survey,
the top three time wasters in business are
ineffective meetings, unclear objectives, and poor
communication among team members.

Map Out Meetings Toward the Box

The advanced way of thinking about an agenda is to visualize it not as a list, but as a *map* guiding the group toward a goal—from where it is to where you want it to be.

Ask yourself, what do I want or need to be different as a result of this meeting? This meeting is taking place to make *what* happen? What is the *goal*?

Here is what a goal is *not*: to talk about something, or to hold discussions on a list of items or topics.

A goal is:

> A decision on the colors in the new logo
>
> A strategy to increase sales

An update is not a goal. It's an update.

A goal is the *product* that your meeting is being conducted to produce. We call it a *product goal*. The secret to improving your meetings is to *map them out backward* from the end goal. Start with your goal, and work backward from there.

The first thing you should do in mapping out your meetings, therefore, is to draw the desired final outcome of the meeting—your product goal—on a flipchart or whiteboard. Draw a big, empty red box almost as large as the entire page. Above the red box, write the goal of the meeting that needs to be filled in. *(Why red? An executive at Facebook told me that when people put a red box around their Facebook ad, it can do 15 percent better; they are not sure why. Therefore, I use red.)*

Next, determine who needs to be there. Do not include people in meetings who do not have to be there.

Does anything need to be read or done in advance? Do not make up work. Assign this step only if it is necessary.

If the meeting turns out not to be as important as you originally thought it would be, cancel it. The number one rule for maximizing the efficiency of your meeting time is not to hold unnecessary meetings in the first place.

Finally, build your agenda backward based on what has to happen during the meeting if you are to reach the established goal.

Now that we've established how to map out our meetings, there are many things that we can do to dramatically improve how we conduct those meetings.

What's Your Mandate?

Now that you've made sure everyone at the meeting understands what the goal of the meeting is, the next step is to establish the mandate of the group. What are we here to decide, and can we decide it here and now? What is the authority of the group, and how is that authority connected to the purpose of the meeting? Are we here to collect input for the management who will then make the decision about the topic? Or, are we here to actually make a decision? That is the mandate.

If the mandate of the meeting is to make a decision, the group must decide up front how that decision will be made. If you plan to have people throwing out ideas, brainstorming and sharing viewpoints—and plan to keep narrowing down those ideas until you have a winner—then you must make that clear from the start, at the beginning of the meeting. If you plan on making the final selection from among various solutions by holding a vote, then you need to clarify that up front as well.

"All right guys, I know there are different viewpoints and opinions in the room. That's the reason we asked you to be here. When it comes to decision-making time, and we'll do that in a democratic way, let's agree right now that whatever we decide as a group, we all stand behind. Can we all agree to that?"

By asking participants to sign this mental contract up front, you make it much easier to get a decision through and be done with the meeting without repeating discussions over and over again.

All "decision" meetings—meetings where the mandate is to make a decision—should have at least one cycle of "open up/close down." During the "open up" mode, people are throwing ideas on the table, brainstorming and sharing points of view. As facilitator, you allow participants to influence one another's opinions. The "Around the Room" technique is an effective example of doing this. The goal is to expand the solution space and make everything transparent. Pros and cons see the light of the day, and everyone feels heard—which will come in very important later!

In "close down" mode, you narrow down the field of possible solutions. The fastest way is by simply voting. Give participants one or two votes or points each. You can introduce rules, such as, "no voting for your own idea." You can eliminate ideas one at a time.

Because you started the meeting by having everyone sign the mental contract, you can now come to a final decision that everyone will support. Or, at least, they will support it more than they would have, had they not signed the mental contract.

Product Goal Versus Process Goal

As we've discussed, meetings need to have a goal.

"Oh, please, Bill," you say. "Everyone knows that, right?"

Okay. Well, ask yourself this question: Within the past four weeks, has every meeting you've attended had a goal that was clear to everyone in the meeting from the very start? To quote the famous comic strip line from Pogo, "We have met the enemy and he is us."

In the first example, the goal of that meeting was a process goal. It was to discuss the subject for an hour. In the second example, the goal of the meeting was a product goal. The goal was to reach four specific decisions.

We humans can be very goal-oriented. When we become committed to a goal, little can stop us from reaching it. When we put our minds to it, we can put a person on the moon, climb Mount Everest, and even survive a bikram yoga class that our friend forces us to attend. So when the assumed goal of a meeting is to have a discussion on a topic for one hour, almost nothing can stop us from filling that hour, regardless of whether an hour is really necessary. That is the problem with process goals. We are committed to following the process and going through everything on the agenda until the time runs out.

However, when we set a product goal for our meetings, we can use that same goal-oriented determination to our advantage. We will be just as determined to reach those four decisions if that is the goal we set for ourselves.

Meetings should have product goals, not process goals. The goal of your meeting should never be to discuss a topic. You should discuss a topic during your meeting to reach the goal of that meeting.

How a Goal Is Different from a Strategy

Roberto is the owner of a restaurant that is only breaking even—no profit, no loss. This is not good, so he decides to meet with his managers and leadership team to discuss how they can improve profit margins. He tells his team that he must see a profit of at least 10 percent after expenses, so he has decided to cut the number of cooks from four to three and reduce the waitstaff from six to five during the evenings.

The meeting starts off slowly because Roberto's team is now a little in shock, and the managers grow quiet as Roberto tells them that they have to fire staff members. They push back a little, telling Roberto that not having enough chefs and waitstaff could cause a lot of problems. They ask Roberto if they could focus on increasing sales and customers instead. Ultimately, Roberto puts his foot down. He moves the discussion to the subject of choosing which staffers should be let go, and he picks one cook and one waiter to fire. The managers leave the meeting feeling terrible, and so does Roberto, frustrated that his managers don't understand business.

In this scenario, what was the goal of the meeting, and what was the strategy?

The goal was to make the restaurant 10 percent profitable. Let's think of the goal as the top of a mountain. The top of a mountain is a fixed location. It doesn't move. The goal of your meeting should be clear, firm, and not up for debate. Roberto did not deviate from his intended goal.

What was the strategy?

There are many terrific books on this topic and different ways to think about goals and strategies, but for now, consider the *goal* to be the top of the mountain, and the *strategy* to be the path to that point. In this case, letting two employees go was Roberto's strategy for reaching his goal. However, there is usually more than one path up a mountain, and there is more than one strategy for reaching your goal. You should use your meeting to identify several strategies and select the best one. Roberto was not open to any other path. When we are stubborn, we turn our strategy into the goal.

What would have made Roberto's meeting more effective?

After Roberto made his goal to increase profits clear, he could have laid out his strategy: laying off two people. He then could have invited the members of his team to brainstorm other options—marketing; sales; more menu items; having staff members hand out free samples on the street to bring people into the restaurant. There are many possibilities.

In real life, running a successful business requires a mix of strategies. Sometimes the best path is to cut costs, and, unfortunately, that can mean cutting staff. Sometimes a better path is to increase revenue and sales. Roberto and his team could have used the meeting to brainstorm marketing and sales ideas, and Roberto could have said, "Okay, let's try these for two months. If they lead to 10 percent profitability, terrific; there's no need to cut positions. If they don't, we can say we tried, and then we'll have to cut the positions."

Roberto's managers would have felt that he had listened to their concerns, and he would have fostered a sense of teamwork. The more your staff members feel like part of a team, the more committed they will be to the business outcomes.

What's the point?

Meetings need to have both goals and strategies, but you have to be very clear on which is which, because confusing the two creates inefficiencies. Many people have one strategy in mind for reaching a goal. It may be a good one, but they subconsciously make that strategy the goal. They are not open to any other paths. Others might allow the discussion of strategies to alter the goal. Either way, the efficiency and productivity of your meetings are undermined.

Be Firm on Your Goal and Flexible on Your Strategies

The goal must be fixed and not up for debate. It is the top of the mountain. Lead, follow, or get out of the way. The strategy is the path up the mountain. There can be more than one path up the mountain, and the discussion of strategies should be fluid and open. There may be some paths that won't get you there, but identifying the best path is the art of business. This is the recipe for productivity in your meetings, and you will be amazed at the breakthroughs you and your staff will have in making decisions and reaching goals.

Climbing Your Mountain

Most people think visually, so flipcharts and whiteboards can be very effective in helping your team visualize goals. Using the sample diagrams, draw a mountain on a flipchart and write your goal on top.

As your staff discusses strategies during your meeting, draw those strategies on the chart as paths toward reaching the top of the mountain. Label the paths.

Hand out different-colored Post-it Notes and markers. Ask each person to write the strategy he thinks will work best on his sticky notes, and then have him come up and put his Post-its on the chart.

This is a very visual way to help your team members brainstorm and work toward a decision. You may also ask your team members to pair up or break up into groups and decide as groups or pairs which strategy is best.

We all have ideas. Some of them are bad, some okay, some good, and some great, but we often don't know which ones are which because it's difficult to be objective about our own contributions. (This is normal; we become wedded to our own ideas.) You balance this tendency with brainstorming, gathering ideas from others, and building on one another's ideas rather than making decisions too quickly.

Some Other Things You Can Use to Make Meetings Better

Understanding the difference between a process goal (bad) and a product goal (good), as well as the difference between a goal and a strategy, is the key to a successful meeting because it gives you a clear map for reaching your goal. It will keep your meetings on track and your team focused on reaching that goal. It will eliminate inefficiencies and wasted time. Now it's time for you to put to work all of the techniques for effective public speaking and communication that you have learned. We will briefly review these main techniques to see how they could be applied during a meeting.

How are you going to open your meeting? With a story? A scene? A question? A statistic? Are you going to throw your alligators a problem to chomp on? Open your meeting with an effective opening technique that will engage the people in your audience, lower their filters, paint pictures in their minds, and evoke emotions.

Next, it's time to use audience involvement techniques to pull the people at your meeting into the topic. You already know these:

> **Around the room.** At the beginning, go around the table and ask everyone to give one starter thought, just a half sentence, on the topic at hand. This lowers everyone's filters, gets the whole group engaged, and doubles the effectiveness of the first portion of the meeting. If you have a prop that people can pass around the room while taking their turns, use it.

> **Body polls.** Asking for a show of fingers or thumbs up or down on a key issue can give you valuable data on where everyone is on the subject. It also signals to people that you expect their input during the meeting, and that their opinions matter to you.

Pair up. Asking people to team up to come up with an idea or solution at the beginning of the meeting can help establish teamwork and build consensus early in the process. It also signals to your staff members that you are expecting their active participation.

Assign jobs. Having individuals serve as timekeeper and note taker keeps the meeting on target and running smoothly. It also increases your audience members' investment in the meeting because they are now actively involved in conducting it.

Closing thoughts. At the end of the meeting, ask each person to commit to one "action step" that she will take toward achieving the goal of the meeting. Then, go around the room and ask each person for a closing thought—a half sentence describing what she will commit to do and one thing that she thinks was accomplished in the meeting. This ends the meeting with everyone positive and focused.

Tracking action steps and commitments. Assign someone in the room the task of writing down the action step that each person commits to in his closing thought at the end of the meeting. Tracking the action steps is a very effective strategy for keeping people motivated because it keeps it real. The goal gains traction because people know that they will be held accountable.

"John, you've committed to getting this done by the next meeting. Let's put that down. We'll start the next meeting with John's report."

Do you think John's report will be ready by the next meeting?

Little Things That Make Meetings Better

Summarize

We all sometimes go long in our comments. It's natural. We get carried away. We're passionate; we're thinking out loud. Often, when people repeat themselves, it's because they feel that they have not been *heard.* They feel that their words were listened to, but that no one really *heard* them. Regardless of why a person may be going on too long, as the meeting facilitator, you can use the technique of "summarize" in one of two ways.

You can summarize for her.

Vanessa keeps saying, "We should recruit more members. . . ." She keeps repeating herself. You, as the facilitator, should say, "Vanessa, you feel that we should recruit more members." Vanessa nods and then relaxes. Why? She feels that she has finally been heard, so she doesn't need to repeat herself again. Notice that you didn't have to say whether or not you agreed with her. You simply validated her opinion.

You can ask someone to summarize his own thoughts.

Jose is talking long and a bit in circles. You say, "Jose, can you summarize your main point?"

You are not telling him to shut up; you are just telling him to summarize the main point. You say it politely and respectfully. Jose might get offended or feel cut off, but the purpose of the meeting is to get things done, and your job, as the facilitator, is to keep things moving. We can all get carried away sometimes. There is nothing wrong with that. There is also nothing wrong with someone interrupting another person and asking for a summary. This is a much more favorable approach than telling someone to stop talking. It gives the person a chance to synthesize his thoughts in a final statement.

Anyone in the meeting can interrupt a speaker and say, "Jose, you lost me; what is your main point?" It doesn't mean we don't love you, just that you lost us.

If you do this, will someone who is being verbose sometimes take offense? Yes. Good. This isn't kindergarten. You are not trying to hurt the person's feelings, but everyone is thinking this and no one else is saying it. You are at least trying to do it in a way that saves the person's face, and you hope that she would do the same for you.

If everyone feels it and no one says it, are we doing that person a favor? Dr. Leo Buscaglia had this great quote. Only someone who loves you tells you when you have goop on your nose. Everyone else lets you walk all day with it.

Why do some people talk too much? There is a mix of good and not-so-good reasons. The good reasons are that they are enthusiastic, have a lot to say, and are genuinely passionate. The not-so-good reasons: they are a bit in love with the sound of their own voices and are not actively listening. They aren't bad people—they just don't read the room well.

You can't fix these "talkers" or call them out on the spot. It's better to redirect their energy. Assign them a job or do something else to channel their energy in a way that helps you and involves everyone else.

I used to be one of these people (and still am from time to time). I monopolized the conversation. If someone had told me, "Bill, you are talking too much; let other people talk," he would have been exactly right, but it would have been hard for me to hear, and unless it was done very skillfully and with humor, it probably would have created a strange dynamic in the meeting.

Sidebars

Twenty students from the student government organization are meeting to plan an event to commemorate the history of the school. One student gives some information about the school's early history that another student disputes. The two have a little argument or discussion about it. However, the debate doesn't matter much to the rest of the group, which is now sitting around waiting for the meeting to get back on track.

Fortunately, the meeting facilitator says to the two arguing students, "Why don't you sidebar that and discuss it during the break?"

They agree, and the meeting continues.

Sometimes a meeting naturally devolves into a discussion between two or three people that does not include the whole group. Here, the facilitator or anyone else in the meeting can ask for a sidebar.

Sidebar is a legal term for a conference during a court trial in which the judge and the lawyers discuss a point of law privately, without the entire courtroom hearing them. The side of the wooden ledge next to the judge's raised seat is the "bar," so the judge can say,

"Sidebar," and the two lawyers will come to that side of the bar for a short, private discussion. When the discussion is concluded, the trial resumes.

In business, the idea of a sidebar is not to kill the discussion, but to have the two or three people engaged in it have the discussion separately, not while the rest of the meeting is being held up waiting for them. The two parties can be asked to report the results of the sidebar back to the boss, facilitator, or group.

Start on Time

Timing can be either a virtuous or a vicious circle. Set the tone of your meeting by beginning on time. Even if some people aren't there when you start, you will get a reputation for starting on time, and people will begin to show up a couple of minutes early in the future. If you wait until everyone gets there, just to be polite, then people will know that and think that they can arrive a little late because the meetings don't always start on time.

At the beginning of the meeting, clarify the goal and the agenda with the group—not to the group.

Propose some time parameters for each part of the agenda, but then be flexible on them. Ask the group not just to approve the agenda, but also for ideas to improve it. If people say, "Let's make this section a few minutes longer or this section shorter," that is very good—it engages the group and increases people's ownership of the outcome of the meeting. If you are not asking the group to improve the agenda and improve the strategy, then you are driving the agenda too much. That means that you don't really need the group on this topic, so you didn't need the meeting.

However, remember to remain firm on the goal. You are allowing the group members to contribute to the agenda, and you are flexible and open on possible strategies to reach the goal. But the goal remains fixed.

Kurt: Do you have any tips for assigning roles during virtual meetings? My team is co-located throughout the region, so we usually meet by phone. How can you involve them over the phone?

Coach: Great question. I'll give you one tip. We all have gone through this process. Before the first conference call we were ever on, we were ready. We had our agenda printed out, with blank sheets available to take notes on. Then we discovered the most magic button ever invented on the phone, called the . . .

Participants: Mute!

Coach: Love that mute button! So we know that everyone is multitasking, and the way to channel the energy of multitaskers is to give them a . . .

Peter: Task.

Coach: Exactly. Give them a task, a job. Let's say you have to present your strategy in five minutes. Say, "I am going to go through our strategy in five minutes. Then I am going to ask each person on the phone to give me at least one idea on how to make our strategy better."

What will happen?

Kurt: They will listen a lot more.

Coach: Why?

Kurt: They need to give an idea. They need to hear the strategy to give ideas about it.

Coach: You have given the audience a job. The alligators get some meat.

Icebreakers

Icebreakers are fun because they create energy, drop filters, and can get people laughing and thinking. Use the best one for the occasion. Some can be very simple; others are more complex. They can be serious or silly, but silly is a lot more fun.

We can use any of our audience involvement techniques as an opening icebreaker, but here's one that I learned from a friend of mine, executive trainer Jim Mustacchia, called "the Lion, the Samurai, and the Grandmother."

This game is played like Rock, Paper, Scissors. First, ask the people in your audience if they are all familiar with that game. Then explain the difference. We act it out with three characters. For the first part, everyone finds a partner. (If your group has an odd number, you can be someone's partner.) Once everyone is ready, instruct the pairs to stand back to back. Then ask each person to decide secretly if she is going to be a lion, a samurai, or a grandmother. At the count of one, two, three—go!—the players whip around to face their partner, showing the gesture of their character.

> Lion roars with claws out: roar!

> Samurai swings down with the sword, killing the lion: hay-yah!

> Grandmother leans in and scolds the samurai with her finger: "Nah, nah, nah!"

According to the rules of the game, the samurai kills the lion, the lion eats the grandmother, and the grandmother scolds the samurai.

After one or two rounds, you move up to a team round where the pairs are combined into larger teams. Depending on the size of your group, you can have multiple teams. The teams huddle together to choose their character. Everyone on the team must be the same character. Then, all the teams pair up to play against each other, and by eliminating the losing teams, you will wind up with a championship round between the last two remaining teams. You can have consolation rounds among the losing teams, and tiebreakers.

The Quiet Ones

Just because someone at a meeting is quiet doesn't mean that he doesn't have something to say. In fact, he may have a very valuable contribution to make, but he doesn't speak up for a variety of reasons. It's important to keep an eye on individuals. If someone is not speaking, but you notice an expression form on her face during the discussion, ask for her thoughts in a gentle, nonconfrontational way.

"Melissa, what do you think of this?"

For example, suppose there are nine people in the meeting and, 20 minutes into it, three of them (Huey, Dewey, and Louie) haven't said a word, always deferring to everyone else. To draw them in, while Guillermo is talking (again), interrupt him and say, "Guillermo, why do you feel that way? And then I am going to ask Huey, Dewey, and Louie what they think about this question. I want to make sure we are hearing from everyone."

Here, we asked Guillermo to summarize and gave the other three a heads-up—a few seconds to collect their thoughts and prepare—while sending the message to the group that everyone has to play.

You don't need to have everyone contribute equally, but everyone needs to contribute from time to time. You can go a long way toward meeting this need by using audience involvement techniques like starter thoughts and other approaches. Not only do these techniques get everyone to talk, but once the ice is broken people are more likely to speak on their own.

Veronika: I have a problem in meetings.

Coach: Go on.

Veronika: (*sighs*) In a lot of meetings, I feel like I'm not a player. Half the meeting goes by, and I will not have said anything. Sometimes I think of something good to say, but it's too late; the subject has changed.

Coach: And that makes you withdraw even more.

Veronika: Exactly. Other people say these really smart or witty things.

Coach: So what is your question?

continued

Veronika: Do you have any tips on how I can be viewed more as a player?

Coach: First, everyone assumes that the way to be a star in meetings is to make brilliant comments, but you actually influence a meeting more with brilliant questions.

In a courtroom, who controls the conversation more, the lawyer asking the questions or the witness giving the answers?

Veronika: The lawyer.

Coach: In a television interview, who is more in control, the reporter asking the questions or the celebrity or person answering them?

Veronika: The reporter.

Coach: So here is your homework. Are you ready? During the next three meetings you are in, I want you to interrupt the meeting with a question during the first few minutes. I don't care what the question is. It can be about logistics, process, product, anything.

Veronika: For example?

Coach: It could be a simple question: "Does everyone have an agenda?" It could be a substantive question. If the leader of the meeting is going through content ABC, and A and B are clear, but you are not completely sure what is behind C, you can interrupt and ask, "Can you say a little more about C?"

Veronika: Say a little more?

Coach: Yes. There are certain short questions that work very well to help the speaker expand on what he is saying: "Say more about that." "What's behind that?" "Why is that?" If you interrupt with a question, are you helping the speaker or hurting him?

Veronika: I don't know.

Coach: Usually, it helps him. You are asking him for more of his own opinion, and most people like that. And are you helping or hurting the audience?

Veronika: If I have a question, others may have the same question.

Coach: But they don't ask it. The person who asks is the one who is viewed as a player.

Veronika: Ahh . . .

Coach: It's like team sports. If one or two players always make the plays and no one else touches the ball, the others are not viewed as players. Until you speak in a meeting, you are sometimes not viewed as a player in that meeting. When you speak, you become one. You've touched the ball.

Veronika: And even a simple question helps break the ice.

Coach: It helps other people, but the main reason to do it is for you. Your questions and comments help get you into the flow. Do you accept your homework? During the next three meetings, will you interrupt in the first few minutes with any kind of question? The more you do it, the better your questions will get.

Veronika: I promise.

Coach: Promise isn't good enough. My little daughter, Anna, says that if you really promise, you have to pinky-swear. (*holds out pinky*) Send me an e-mail after those three times and tell me, in just a line or two, how well it worked. Pinky-swear?

Veronika: (*holding out pinky*) Pinky-swear!

Socializing

As much as people may dread meetings, they often don't mind the chance to chat and get caught up with coworkers or colleagues, or the chance to get to know their clients better on a personal level. Business is all about relationships, and a quick discussion about a client's children or a customer's golf swing can help strengthen those relationships. However, many people in business frown on this form of socializing, seeing it as a waste of time. Others are confused as to what is proper social conversation in business situations. If you are running a meeting, you need to know how to strike the proper balance between allowing people to socialize and keeping the meeting on time and on track.

I will often ask someone, "How's business?"

I consider it a social question within the work sphere, just as I might ask, "How's life?" in a purely social context. When I ask, "How's business?" the answer is usually, "Oh, busy." When I ask, "Good busy or bad busy?" the person has to think for a moment. That kicks off a brief but high-quality conversation that gives me a chance to hear how things are with that person and gives her the opportunity to do the same for me. It's not wasted time. It's social, but it's often also efficient because it's a quick way to bring the most relevant information to the surface, and it is based on sincere curiosity.

Werner: Isn't socializing just a nicety? A waste of time that could be used for real business?

Coach: What do you think?

Werner: Honestly, I think it is, most of the time, but what do you think?

Coach: What is your dream car?

Werner: My dream car?

Coach: Yes, your dream car, if you could have any one for free.

Werner: A Lamborghini . . . bright, bright red! (*laughter*)

Coach: Okay. You get a brand-new one, and we will throw in the sunglasses, too, to complete your look. (*laughter*) You are driving it off the lot with a full tank of gas but no oil in the engine. What happens?

Eric: Gas but no oil? It would stall.

Coach: Anyone disagree?

Christian: No, it would run.

Coach: Correct. You could get on the autobahn and fly, but after a while what happens?

Christian: It breaks down.

Coach: Eventually, yes, but why? What is happening in the engine?

Harold: It overheats.

Coach: Why does it overheat?

Harold: The friction can get so bad that it can actually start to melt the engine block over time if there is no oil.

Coach: So what does the oil do for the engine?

Harold: It reduces friction.

Coach: Exactly. Friction is part of the energy. You need it, just as you need creative tension in any team. But too much friction damages the engine. The oil reduces it to safe levels.

In business, socializing can have a number of purposes. It can create a stronger connection between us, which lowers filters. It can reduce friction enormously, but there can be too much. Just as an engine needs just liters, not gallons, of oil, we don't need to go sailing with our colleagues every weekend in order to work well together. It's your call to assess how much is enough and what the right mix is for optimum performance.

Some of the most rewarding e-mails that we get back after Own the Room courses are about the impact the training has had on meetings. Participants will write us that their 60-minute meetings are now 45 minutes, and that they're getting more done in that time.

The e-mails are always different. We have received e-mails telling us that the red boxes have reduced decision making to 10 minutes, that meetings are routinely only 30 or 40 minutes, that clients now use checklists to fill the boxes, and so forth. In some e-mails, clients will tell us that it took time for their staffs to adapt to the change in how they run meetings and to learn how to use techniques like summarize, sidebar, and the red boxes. Some will tell us that adopting the techniques were more effective because several staff members went through the training together. But, all of the e-mails tell us that the training made a big difference on the efficiency and productivity of meetings.

SUMMARY

★ Map out meetings backward from the goal.

★ The goal of your meeting should be a product goal, not a process goal.

★ A strategy is not a goal, but one path—usually one of several, if not many—for reaching a goal.

★ Be flexible on strategy, but fixed on the goal.

★ Keep meetings on track and in focus by using sidebars and summarizing to guide the discussion.

★ Sparing a little time for icebreakers and socializing can be very helpful in building relationships and fostering teamwork.

★ Apply the same opening, closing, and audience involvement techniques you have learned for public speaking to running meetings.

CHAPTER 20

Leveraging Powerful Panels

To be good is expected. To be better is the challenge.
—CHRISTI PEDRA

E very now and then, you may attend a terrific panel where sparks fly because of great content and great personalities, but just as often, panels tend to be a Frankenstein's monster of great people, nice sponsors, industry big shots, and disparate content stapled together by the personality of the moderator.

How effective, on average, would you say that these panel presentations are? Most people would say that most panels are not great, even when they have great people, so let's look at why that is and how to improve it.

Panels often start with redundancy. Even though we already have all the panelists' bios in front of us in a nice brochure or folder or handout, the moderator is compelled, by a normal human instinct, to add value. She offers a creative introduction for each person on the panel, even though the panelists have already been praised by their own (self-written) bios. Then, after this nice welcome by the moderator, what do most panelists tend to do?

They introduce themselves again and offer more credentials.

Why?

We're human. Maybe some psychologist could help us understand this. I do know that when I was in my early twenties and first started

233

speaking, I was the very same way or probably worse. I would pretend not to care, but the truth is, I did. I would try to make sure that the moderator mentioned certain things about me in his introduction. We all have a strong need to build ourselves up. (Realizing that this is healthy and normal helps you understand even more deeply why, when you make the audience the star, you've *got it*. People are happy when they are recognized.)

As we have developed the Own the Room training system and created these techniques, there have been countless moments when I have realized, "Aw, man, I need to take our advice again." The matter of being introduced was one of those breakthroughs. I had to stop caring about myself. I haven't been introduced in years. When someone asks me how I want to be introduced, I say, "Here's Bill."

It's not that I don't want the people in the audience to know who I am, but I've learned that they will get to know me, little by little, as we go along. Forcing more information on an audience up front doesn't make the people in it get to know me better, or even faster. It also does not enhance the effectiveness of my presentation. However, I need to know *them*. I need to make them the star. Knowing the people in my audience and making them the star is crucial to my presentation. So, whether I'm on a panel or moderating or doing a keynote, I almost always start with audience involvement techniques—a body poll, a pair-up, then setting a scene. A body poll, a pair-up, then a scene. This approach always works.

For better or for worse, the bar for panel presentations is not set very high. You can apply many of the techniques you've already learned to use in other settings to allow you to stand out from the crowd easily and make your contribution to the discussion memorable and effective.

Who Are You?

Sometimes I hear, okay, but the audience does need to know who I am, right? I agree. On the rare occasion when the audience, for whatever reason, does not already know who you are, you can just slip it in. Let's say your name is Jacob, you're on the panel, and you make a provocative statement. You follow the statement with a confused look on your face, and say, "All right, Jacob, what does that mean exactly?"

You just did a few things at once. You slipped in your own name as if the audience were talking to you. You pre-raised a question that you knew was on people's minds already, and you used some body language to connect with the audience.

Every once in a while, slip in your name and ask yourself a question, as if you were the audience.

Similarly, let's say you have a relevant and also impressive credential or life experience—a master's or doctoral degree in a related topic. If you give that credential up front, it can be perceived as bragging, or you may come across as insecure. Waiting for a relevant moment to share this information gives that biographical information more power. It's called a "reveal." You just slip it in.

"I once spent a few years in Los Angeles, Westwood actually, studying until UCLA said, 'Okay, you have enough credits, here's your doctorate; you can get out of here now.' I loved my time there, and one of the things (*pivoting toward a more serious tone*) I learned was that . . . ," and you slip in your fact that's relevant to the topic.

Be Different

Microsoft founder Bill Gates has done many things in his life that you could say no one else has done in business and philanthropy. One of them has been to put significant resources into global health issues, including an initiative to fight the spread of malaria in poor countries. Malaria is carried and spread by mosquitoes, and several years ago, when Bill was discussing the disease before a large audience at a TED conference, he released a jar of mosquitoes into the audience. (He later assured the audience that they did not carry the malaria virus.)

Do you think he got the audience's attention? Do you think he made his point? Do you think the people in his audience remembered his presentation?

I am always asked to give "just my number one tip" for delivering a great presentation. And I always answer, "Easy. Identify and eliminate weak language. Nothing else will have as great an impact on improving your communication." At that point, eyes start to roll, and I am asked, "Okay, so what is number two?"

My answer: "Something almost as powerful: be *different*."

Do something different that no one else has done.

Each time.

This alone brings tremendous results. Just ask yourself what you can do that no one else has done. That's it. Reach for those three centimeters to access all kinds of crazy ideas. Just pick one and do it. Reach up and break through the clutter. To be memorable and effective and to have an impact, you have to be a little more outrageous and creative than the other guy.

When you do come up with your unusual and creative idea, think of it like triage. About 10 percent of the time, it will work. Gold. Magic. Wow. Where did that come from? A rush. Another 10 percent of the time, it will be bronze. Not great, but give yourself a pat on the back for having had the courage to try it.

The other 80 percent of the time? Silver. It will *sort of* work. You'll get some good feedback. A few tweaks here and there, and it can become gold next time.

When you combine the courage to keep trying new things with demanding and being open to feedback, you create an almost unstoppable trajectory of growth. Adopting a mindset in which you are fearless about trying your own new ideas and tweaking them until they work is the secret in the secret sauce. Since we are "revealing" secrets, perhaps you are realizing one of mine now. Everyone thinks that my training makes people better speakers and presenters. That's not actually what I do. I am teaching you how to be your own professional public speaking coach, to be able to teach yourself what works and why it works, piece by piece. Your improvement is just a symptom of your becoming a coach. You are a professional speaking coach right now—you don't even have to wait until you've finished the book and all the exercises. It's true. If you had to teach a class on how to give powerful presentations, you could do it right now. As a coach, your number one client is always yourself. Coach yourself to try your own ideas, and the magic will happen.

> *Relationship tip.* Build bridges between yourself and the other panelists before and after you speak, and look for ways to mention them during your presentation or answers that make them look good. The more you make others the star, the more brightly you shine.

Use Your Bag of Tricks

Whether you are speaking on a panel, delivering a keynote address, or moderating the panel, the same techniques you have learned that make you effective in other situations apply to these settings. Open with a scene or a story; eliminate weak language; use strong language to paint pictures and evoke emotion; engage the audience members with audience involvement techniques. Some of these techniques are particularly helpful to you as a panelist or moderator when you have very limited time to connect with your audience.

Openings

Using the imagine technique to pull your audience into a scene helps you connect with your audience very quickly. Whether you set a scene, tell a story, or open with a question or a statistic, make sure the opening connects the audience to your topic and points the audience in the direction you want it to go.

Involving the Audience

Audience involvement techniques, like body polls and pair-up, can be *especially* effective in helping moderators elevate their panel to a higher level. It's almost like they are made for panels. If you are moderating a panel, and you do a quick but different audience involvement technique—maybe take one minute before each speaker—you elevate the whole event, and your audience and your panelists will be impressed.

For example, suppose you are moderating a panel on digital media, and the first speaker has just wrapped up his discussion of the latest trend in Internet advertising. Before you give the floor to the second speaker, you conduct a quick body poll of the audience:

"Show me, using thumbs up or thumbs down, if you think this trend is going to continue for the next year."

Or:

"Show me, using your fingers, on a scale from zero to ten, how concerned you are about your company being able to keep up with the changing digital environment."

Not only do *you* see the results, but so does everyone else. People can look around and see what everyone else is thinking. The answers give you information, which is like clay. *Do something* with the clay. Comment on what you're noticing in people's answers, or ask them what they've noticed in others' answers. Make a serious comment, make a joke, or ask the audience to comment. Ask the outliers to explain to the group why they feel the way they do.

If, as a panelist or moderator, you were to opt for a pair-up or pair-and-share technique, you would pair audiences into teams of two, assign a simple task, and then ask the small teams to share their results with the whole group.

For example, you would say:

"When I say, 'Go,' turn to your partner. You have 30 seconds to . . ."

Closing Thought or Commitment

One of the strongest closings you have available to you, as a panel moderator or keynote speaker, is to ask the audience members to say out loud what action they will commit to take on the topic you have been discussing. If the group is small, you can go around the room and ask each person to say what he is going to do. If it is a large group, like a conference, you can use the pair-and-share technique and ask the audience members to tell the person next to them what action they are committing to take. It doesn't matter whether one person hears them or the whole group does. Saying the commitment out loud makes it more likely that someone will follow through.

Like all of these techniques, this is rather simple to do, and it will feel easy after you do it a couple of times, so the art becomes the actual question itself.

The Possibilities of Social Media

The integration of social media into our culture provides you with a range of audience involvement techniques that we did not have only a few years ago. Imagine that you are moderating a panel at a large conference and you wrap up the event this way:

"Okay, when I say, 'Go,' and not until I say, 'Go,' I want everyone to stand up and pick a partner that you already know. At least one of you must have a smartphone. Let me repeat. Pick someone you already know, but make sure that one of you has a smartphone. Ready, go."

Now for part two:

"Now, this is going to be a gentle competition. When I say, 'Begin' —and *do not start* until I say, 'Begin'—you are going to, one, take your partner's photo; two, title it with one sentence, no more, on the topic of the day; and three, post it on any social media platform, I don't care which. I will ask in a moment *what* you said and *where* you posted it. As soon as you are both done, have a seat. We'll see who finishes first and last. Ready, begin!"

What would happen? It would be pure pandemonium, but it would be memorable. Everyone would be thinking about the topic. Everyone would get to be the star, producer, writer, and director, and it would work no matter how many people are in the audience.

TWEETING ALERT

Remember that anything you say can be tweeted or posted, in or out of context. Find words and phrases that paint the pictures you want to convey, and reinforce your message so that people will remember what you said and want to post or tweet what they heard from you. Be careful of language that can be twisted against your goals, and avoid flippant answers to difficult questions, even in jest.

SUMMARY

★ Let's try it for real. Take out your smartphone and go to Facebook. Enter "Own the Room" and find the group with thousands of likes. Press like. Then add a comment about this book.

★ Be different. You can use all the techniques you have learned for openings, closings, and audience involvement as a panel member or moderator.

★ Refrain from introducing yourself in the first sentence. You have probably been introduced to the panel audience several times by the time you get your chance to speak.

★ Build relationships with other members of the panel by including them in your segment. The more you make others the star, the more you shine.

CHAPTER 21

Become a Motivational and Keynote Speaker

Make sure you have finished speaking
before your audience has finished listening.
—DOROTHY SARNOFF

Many years ago, while I was volunteering with the organization Do Something, with my friends Andrew Shue and Michael Sanchez, Andrew and I wrote a short public service announcement, about President Teddy Roosevelt, to be read and videotaped by President Bill Clinton. President Clinton read over the material once in just seconds and delivered it to the camera with amazing skill.

I am often asked if people like President Clinton are just natural-born speakers, and if just a few lucky people are born with that ability. While I would say that of course people like President Clinton or President Reagan are definitely blessed with outstanding communication abilities, I have had the opportunity to work with many politicians from both sides of the aisle, and . . . no one is born doing a keynote speech. Whatever ability a person has, it comes from learning and mastering certain techniques. This is true for all great speakers. *All* of them. *You* too can become a great, natural-looking speaker. All of us have the potential to be good, some of us very good, and some great. All of us can be better. You just have to put in the work. It can happen faster than you think.

There is *no* one big thing in communication. It's all the *little* things that add up to big impact. Any cognitive skill can feel overwhelming while we are learning it, but think of all the times you have already done this over the course of your life. One of the hardest and most amazing things—if you think about it and how much it involves—any human being can learn to do is walk. But we all learned. We tried and fell, tried and fell. Now we can do it without thinking. We go through the same steps when we learn other cognitive skills. All of us followed the same process when we learned to ride a bike: *"Daddy, don't let go; I can't do it! Don't let go. Oh, wow, I can do it! Did you see me?!"*

All of these things, and so many other skills that we have mastered over the course of our lives, require us to think of a number of things at the same time, and then to practice the skill until we perfect it. Imagine the skill layering into your cognitive brain. However, you have to keep repeating the *correct* technique. Otherwise, you are teaching yourself mediocre skills, or even bad habits. Imagine learning another language. If you are practicing saying new vocabulary words, but you do not pronounce the words very well, then you are becoming more comfortable with the wrong pronunciation, which becomes a habit. The same thing goes for those who are golfers without good technique. "Practice doesn't make perfect. Perfect practice makes perfect."

If learning something new feels overwhelming and frustrating at times, that's how we know we are doing it right. Soon, we will become aware that something just "clicked" in our mind, and we are now performing our new skill like it's second nature. If you've been doing the exercises and following the instructions, you are on your way to mastering some of the techniques. You may be frustrated by others, but it will click.

Here's another secret: there are only two things you need to do to keep improving, even after all this training.

1. Notice little things.

2. Try new things.

That's it.

Alone, either of these is great to have, but together, they make progress unstoppable, like peanut butter and jelly or rice and beans. Did you know that there are enzymes in the rice and beans that are released when those two foods are eaten together that make them more nutritious? I didn't, but they apparently work better together than they do separately.

How do *notice* and *try* go together? If you learn to notice and analyze techniques and how they work on an audience, but you never actually try them, you're obviously not going to improve too much as a speaker. Likewise, if you are always trying new techniques, but you don't take the time to notice and analyze how they did and didn't work with your audience, you won't get much better either. You need both. The more you build your "noticing muscles," combined with your superpowered courage, the more you become the speaking coach, and your number one client will always be yourself.

You walk with two legs; you row a boat with two oars; you think with both sides of your brain. Power and progress start with balance.

The concepts we've covered in this book are actually fairly complicated. We made them easier to process by breaking them down into techniques, tricks, and tips that, as you've now seen, build on each other, spiral, and interconnect, all in the journey toward your becoming the best speaker you can be. We've shown you that learning starts with asking the right questions, accelerates with examples, and solidifies with practice and integration with your own life experiences. Smart people are stubborn learners. You won't own anything unless you see it, come to it, and understand it for yourself.

This brings us to the twin big daddies of public speaking—the motivational speech and the keynote address.

I want you to think of the last keynote speech you sat through. Were you in the audience, or were you watching it on television? Who delivered it? Can you remember what that person said, what you learned, or how it made you feel? In this chapter, we are going to turn you into a highly paid motivational speaker, where you get invited to do the keynote on tour across the country. Just remember, when you go pro, I get 10 percent of all T-shirt sales, deal?

I want you to start by preparing a one-to-two-minute "life lesson" story.

Think of a story about something that really mattered in your life, where you learned a lesson from someone you cared about while you were growing up.

What really matters in life?

It could be something you learned when you were very little, or when you were a teenager. You might have learned it from a parent, grandparent, teacher, coach, relative, or sibling, or from a unique situation. Think about the lesson you learned, how you learned it, and who helped you learn it.

Take a moment and frame out the story—not word for word, but just a block outline. There are probably a very small number of scenes in the story, so let's begin with your first scene.

As we've learned, let's practice starting with a scene. Here are some examples. Remember, starting with a scene means you give no intro or ramp-up (no weak language). Begin by pulling us into the middle of a scene:

> I was eight years old . . . (*holding your hand to measure how tall you were*)

> It was a hot summer day . . .

> My grandmother always wore these green sweaters . . .

When you change scenes, change your position in the room so that it makes sense in the story. If there are three scenes in your story, walk to three different parts of the room or the stage. This makes the story come alive in *three dimensions*:

> The first dimension is your content.

> The second dimension is your voice range and body language with your face and hands.

> The third dimension is your space, the room or the stage. If you cannot move around—if you are on television, at a lectern for

a video call, or sitting in a meeting—that is still your space, and you must use as much of that space as you can in a way that harmonizes with your content. But don't just walk back and forth between two places in the room, unless that is what is happening in the story. Change your scene; change your position.

For example:

> The barn at my uncle's farm was huge—at least it felt that way to me when I was 10 years old and looking up at it. (*There you are standing and looking up like a 10-year-old at a huge barn.*)
>
> And my cousin and I were goofing around, and we fed the horse some grass we had picked, just for fun. Later, at the dinner table with my aunt, I asked where my uncle was, and she said he was out in the barn with the vet because the horse was sick. (*Here, you would be sitting down in a different part of the room, at a table. If you sit* in *the story, sit when you* tell *that part of the story.*)
>
> And, my cousin and I just looked at each other. We pretended we didn't know why the horse was sick.
>
> Later that night, I had to go up to my uncle in the living room and tell him it was me. (*Here, you stand still in a different part of the room, as if you were talking to your uncle.*) I found out later that of course he had known it was us all along, but he didn't accuse me or call me a liar. He waited for me to do the right thing.
>
> The lesson I learned from that—that stayed with me for life—was always to tell the truth. And not to feed anything to animals, except what they are supposed to eat.

Now take a few minutes and frame *your* story. This is a safe space. Record yourself, knowing that you will erase it afterward. Go ahead and film, play, give yourself feedback, and delete.

Now we are going to turn this into a keynote or motivational speech and make you famous.

1. Write down what the main theme or lesson of your story was for you: _____

2. Now reduce that theme to the fewest possible words. Using the horse story as an example . . .

   a. "You should always tell the truth, even when you know you will get in trouble."

      (Good, but too long. Make it shorter.)

   b. "Tell the truth, even when it's hard," or, "Tell the hard truth."

      (Better.)

   c. Now turn the lesson of the story into a bumper sticker. Give it a twist: serious, deep, funny—whatever tells the story. In this example, one possibility (there are many) is, "Let the truth out of the barn."

Your "bumper sticker" has to be unique, different, and tied to the story—while still being brief. If you feel that your bumper sticker is hokey, don't worry about it. Never underestimate the power of hokey to move an audience.

Great speaking is sometimes about setting up something at one point in the speech that you will come back to later—even if it doesn't quite make sense at the time. So, now that we have the bumper sticker and the frame of the story, let's add three pieces that will give it motivational power. We will put a sentence before your story and two sections after the story to give the story the added dimension it needs if it is to be worthy of a motivational speech or keynote address.

1. Sentence before your story:

   a. Open by standing off to one side and setting up the bumper sticker to return to later. Let's stick with the horse story.

The first words out of your mouth should be: "I'm going to give you a gift of seven words that were given to me, and that I am sharing with you: let the truth out of the barn."

    b. Then step away. They don't know what it means now, but they will later.

2. Tell the story the way you practiced it:

    a. Set up the seven words, your bumper sticker, in the middle. Unveil the words with a pregnant pause.

    b. When you get to the key scene in the middle, slow down and focus:

> After I had confessed, he let me squirm and cry a bit, and then, in his own folksy-wisdom way, he said seven words that stuck with me for the rest of my life. He said, "Next time, Bill, . . . (*pregnant pause of an extra second or two*) *let the truth out of the barn*. Best you learn now; there are always going to be times when it's easier to tell a little lie, but it always ends up hurting someone—most of all, you."
>
> And he walked out.

3. Set a scene illustrating how those words help you now:

    a. After you've told the story, stop and let it sink in. (Don't belabor the point by repeating it.)

    b. Walk to a new spot in the room and say:

> I didn't realize it then, but throughout my life there *have* been times—and there still are—when it feels easier to fib, fudge, or tell an outright lie to avoid unpleasantness. But my uncle was right then, and he's right now. It always ends up hurting someone—most of all, ourselves. We feel sick inside, knowing that we didn't do the right thing.

4. Make your lesson a gift to the people in your audience:

  a. Your story becomes their story, too. Now your seven words are *their* seven words.

  (Step to a new position in the room.)

> So now I want to make these not just my or his words, but a gift to you. The fact is, we all, at one time or another, have seen some truth locked in a barn: a chance we had to face the music, to right a wrong, accept a responsibility, or even tell someone else the truth. What is that barn for you? You can debate that until the cows come home—excuse me, horses come home—but the question is, why not let it out now? The healing can't start until that happens.
>
> Now, the next time you are facing a tough situation where it's easier not to tell the truth, just remember my uncle and those seven words. Say them with me now, "Let the truth out of the barn."

You now have a formula for building a motivational speech—or maybe even an article or a book. So let's start from the beginning and construct your speech.

You have your story to get you started. Now, go back through each step in the chapter and add each piece. When you have completed all the steps—including the one to practice—take out your video camera. Record, play, give feedback. Do so as many times as you want to or you feel are necessary.

I want you to take a moment and think of your biggest *aha!* moment while you were reading this chapter. Say it out loud, and write it down here as well:

_____

_____

SUMMARY

★ No one is born a keynote speaker. All great speakers invest considerable time in practicing and mastering techniques.

★ Notice little things and try new things. You cannot improve unless you try new things and note what works and what doesn't work.

★ A keynote or motivational speech should boil down to a life lesson that can be expressed in a clever "bumper sticker."

CHAPTER 22

Deliver an Elevator Pitch: Selling in Three Easy Steps

*We must have perseverance and, above all,
confidence in ourselves. We must believe that we are gifted
for something and that this thing must be attained.*
—Marie Curie

Think of a product or service that you love. *Really* love. You find yourself recommending it to your family and friends. It could be a:

Website

Restaurant

Gadget

App

Car

Thing for your home

It can be anything at all, as long as you love it so much that you are just a walking commercial for it.

Got one in mind?

Let's take that product that you recommend, and use it to learn how to do an elevator pitch. An elevator pitch is a classic sales technique that is really just a demonstration of how you can sell something in a very short amount of time. If you had a dream customer alone in the elevator with you, and you had only the time it took for the elevator to go from the ground floor to the top of the building to make the most of this captive audience, could you make a successful pitch?

As with most things, there is more than one right way to do an elevator pitch (there's more than one answer to most of life's questions), but here, let's break it into three simple sections. We'll use the product that you like as a case study to practice as we go, and then we'll bring it back to more serious business and practice the technique at the end.

I'm from Michigan, with its many beautiful small lakes, so let's use the simple analogy of fishing. Whether you have never fished or you do it all the time, it will help you visualize how an elevator pitch can work. It's an approach that's called "hook, line, and sinker." To catch the fish, first you have to get the fish to bite the *hook*. You then use the *line* to reel in the fish close to the boat. Finally, you need to *close the deal*: get the fish *into the boat*.

Let's work through an example. I'm going to ask you to apply the technique to your product in a moment, but let's start with a generic example, Amazon.com. (A company with many nice people, I can tell you.)

Hook: What Problem Does the Product Solve? Create a Scene

What problem or problems does Amazon solve? Here is where you start to discipline your thinking for sales. If you say, "It's easy; there's lots of selection," you are already blowing your pitch. Those statements are true, but they are not problems. (They'll be part of the line to reel the client in, but they are not the hook.)

What problem(s) might exist for you that Amazon can solve? Think for a second.

> I have to buy stuff as gifts, and it's hard to figure out what people want.

I don't have a lot of time for (or patience with) shopping.

How do you keep your credit card info safe?

These are problems that need to be solved. Now let's turn these problems into a small scene. This is where you and I will start to become like the schmaltzy but effective infomercial spokespersons we see at two o'clock in the morning on television.

> It's right before the holidays, and you are frustrated. You're circling the mall parking lot, trying to find a spot to park. The kids in the backseat are fighting. You finally get into the mall and find the store where you want to buy that thing for your spouse, and the store has run out. We've all had our shopping challenges, right?

If the people in your audience nod, even a little, or agree with their eyes, *that* is when you set the hook. How do you know when you have set the hook? Their faces and eyes will tell you when they can relate to the frustration. They say something like, "Yeah, I have been there," or, "That *would* be frustrating."

One-third of the elevator pitch is done.

I was lucky enough to once be at a dinner with Howard Schultz, founder of Starbucks. At one point in the conversation, I don't remember the context, someone said to Howard, "Well, you sell coffee, so..." Howard interrupted and said, "No, no... we don't sell coffee. We sell *atmosphere*." There was the secret of Starbucks's success. I am not a coffee drinker. I know from my wife and friends that Starbucks does make pretty awesome coffee products, but what it really sells is so much more than that. Think. What are you selling?

Now it's your turn to practice the hook. Get out your video camera (or your smartphone, tablet, laptop, or a full Hollywood film crew; you pick).

Take your "product" and create a hook. Film yourself, but don't erase it yet. I don't want *any* of the line yet. No features. Don't even *mention* the product yet, *just* the hook. Think of the problems the product solves, and turn those problems into a small scene. You have permission to exaggerate a wee bit, and I want you to channel your inner infomercial salesperson. (Don't underestimate the power of schmaltzy.)

Leave that on the video for now, and let's learn how to do the line.

Line: Pre-answer Questions

Pre-answer any questions (possible objections) that the people in your audience might have, in rapid succession, before they even can think of them. You answer these questions by discussing the product's features.

Now that the fish has bitten the hook, you have to reel it in toward the boat. Most fish will resist, and most people will resist trying something new. They will have natural and healthy objections that will have to be overcome. The purpose of the *line* is to pre-answer those questions (objections and concerns) in the order, more or less, in which they might pop up in the audience's mind.

In the Amazon.com example, what might some reasonable objections or concerns be for people who have never used Amazon?

It's not safe.

I can't trust my credit card information to anyone.

It's probably more expensive.

You can't look at different sizes or try on clothing.

You can never know exactly what concerns people are going to have or in what order they will have them. But, for the line part of the pitch, we make our best guess and pre-answer what we think those objections might be. We do this quickly, in order to flip these questions and objections from possible weaknesses into probable strengths.

For example:

> Amazon solves all those problems. It's fast, it's completely safe,
> and it has better prices because it has a much wider selection.
> You can even see the different sizes and colors on-screen and
> read customer reviews. It's not perfect, but what is? It was so
> much easier than I thought it would be, and now I use it a lot.

See what I did? I didn't wait for people to raise their objections
and then overcome them one at a time. In an elevator pitch, you address the objections before the person even thinks of them.

How do you know when you are done?

It's the same as the hook. The eyes of the audience—whether it's
one person or a big group—will tell you. When you see an expression
on someone's face or in his eyes that says, "Hmm. Interesting," or,
"Curious," that is when you switch to the close, the *sinker*.

Okay, now back to your video. This time, pick up where you left
off with the hook and film *just* the line. You could start with, *"And
that's what I love about (name of product). It . . ."*

Become your infomercial salesperson, going live to millions of
people. Film your line now.

One mistake a number of us make in sales is continuing to sell
when someone has already "bought." This is a place where you can
lose something that you already have. Now that you have people interested, you have to *clos*e the deal. You have the fish up close to the
boat; you are two-thirds of the way there, but you still have to get the
fish into the net. Otherwise, all of your work is lost. Don't let the fish
wriggle off the hook here.

Now for the last step, the *sinker*.

Sinker: Close the Deal with an Action Step and Ask for a Commitment

There are different ways to close, but the one we will practice here is to
ask the audience members for a commitment that you then have them

communicate to you. One of the most powerful motivators we ever have driving us is having made a commitment to our peers. Therefore, you want to ask the people in your audience to commit to a *small step* that is super-easy to do and that they are very *likely* to do (which increases your influence). You don't want to ask them for a big step that, realistically, they probably won't do (which undercuts your influence). A baby step that everyone does is much more powerful than a giant step that no one does. Completing the Amazon example:

> I want you to make me a promise. My five-year-old says that "stronger than a promise is a pinky-swear, Daddy." So I want you all to hold up your pinky and pinky-swear that the next time you need to shop for something online, you will go to Amazon first. Just for a couple of minutes, poke around and look at things. If you don't see anything you like, fine. You tried it; you didn't see anything you wanted to buy; no problem. But you go to Amazon first. When you have to buy something, you say, "Oh, yeah, I pinky-swore to Bill that I would at least try Amazon first, so let me check it out." Okay, everyone, show me the pinky. (*looking each person in the eye*)

You will note I didn't actually *sell* anything on Amazon. I just secured a promise to go look, a commitment to a next step. This is important in any selling process, but especially in an elevator pitch. If you work, say, for the global engineering and industrial firm Siemens, and you are selling wind farms, the potential client is not going to write you a check in the elevator. You cannot complete the whole sales process in a minute, so your goal is simply to get to a reasonable next step: a meeting, a demo, a sample, or a promo video that the person agrees to watch—whatever you think will best move the sale forward.

Your turn.

You have already filmed the hook and the line. Now film the sinker and close the deal. Sell some product, baby! Get your audience to commit to *some* action. When you are done, watch all three steps in a row. You just did your first elevator pitch.

As you watch yourself, demand feedback from yourself. You are well trained now to always, always, always start with the positive. What are three things you did well? Which of the three stages was your strongest? Why? Which phrases did you deliver that were particularly effective, that landed? Why?

What is one thing that you could have done better? What was the weakest part? If you lost the fish, where did you lose it? Go ahead and delete the evidence now.

I want you to do one more pitch with the same product, building on your own feedback. Remember, move on to the next stage as soon as the last stage is set, but no sooner. The more you exaggerate in practice, the faster the skill will be integrated into your neural pathways. Taking a point to a bit of an extreme can produce extremely good results. Don't be intellectual. *Become* the character we see at 2:00 in the morning selling mops.

Okay, take two. Do your whole elevator pitch, all three stages. Film, play, demand feedback, and delete. Go sell us an idea!

One of the keys to effective sales is for *you* to believe you are doing *them* a favor. If *you* don't have a GPS and *I* get you to buy one, you are not doing me a favor, *I* am doing *you* a favor. Of course, if I am a GPS manufacturer and you buy one from me, we both win. You have to believe that *you are helping them*. They *really are going to enjoy* that restaurant, that app, or that vacation place. Believing allows you to be much more bold and passionate in your approach.

Bill Gates has famously said that his goal was neither to build a giant company nor to make a billion dollars. His goal was to put a personal computer in every home. Microsoft doesn't even manufacture computers! Bill *believed*. Do you have a personal computer in your home?

What allows me to be bold in asking you to do all these silly exercises and learn new techniques? I know, from watching so many people benefit from our training, how much this will improve your public speaking, communication, and leadership skills, and how much more enjoyable these elements of your work life will be for you. I *believe* that it will make you much more successful in achieving your own goals. That belief emboldens me.

You have the basics; now it's just practice. As always, the best people to practice on are the innocent people in your private life. Practice on your friends and your family. Sell them on an idea or anything you like. But practice the *steps* in the right order. Watch their faces and their eyes to know when to advance.

Now please respond out loud, using good voice modulation and body language, to this question: "What was one of your key lessons from this chapter?"

After you have said it out loud, please write your answer here:

_____

_____

SUMMARY

★ Practicing an elevator pitch allows you to home in on the essence of your product and your story.

★ A product isn't sold on its features, but on the problems that those features solve for the customer. Ask yourself, what am I selling?

★ One of the keys to effective sales is for *you* to believe that *you* are doing *your customer* a favor, not the other way around.

Practice

Now that you have the basics and feel for an elevator pitch, let's apply it to a more serious part of your business. Take something that you need to sell in your real work. It could be a product or service, an idea, or a process. Imagine an audience that you would need to sell it to—whether it be a person or a group—and determine exactly what you want that audience to do or commit to do by the end. Then frame it briefly, make an outline if you want, and then videotape yourself doing that pitch. Play, give feedback, and delete.

A Final Word

★

There is no *one* moment that defined my journey as a communicator. There were *many*.

This moment is for *you*. It's a moment to stop, think, and ponder. Now you are the coach, and your number one client is yourself.

Think of your whole story. Let's track your communication skill over your whole life. Hold the book in one hand and put your other hand out and down. That was you when you were born. Wow, you were cute. Then move your hand a little to the right. Your skill improved a lot when you mastered this whole words thing, and over the next few years, you became a bit of a chatterbox. (My friend Paul Begala has a funny way of looking at this as a parent. He says, "The first year, you can't wait for them to say their first word and take their first step. For the next 17 years, you are trying to get them to sit down and be quiet.") As your hand moves up through your lifetime, you see where you've had little and big jumps in skill and passion and where you were on a plateau.

Now you have taken some big steps up and are at this moment. Remember Yogi Berra's famous saying: "When you get to the fork in the road, take it." You've absorbed some knowledge, learned new tools and techniques, and—depending on how much you have been practicing already—seen some growth. You can stay on this new plateau just by practicing occasionally. You may backslide if you don't practice.

Or you can keep taking the path of continuous enjoyment and continuous improvement. Notice little things. Try new things. Believe. Affirm yourself and your own style. Your personality and your sense of humor are perfect for you. You are *always* the perfect you in each of your presentations.

What is the single biggest thing you can do (besides getting structured training in a class)? The answer is easy: demand feedback in real life. The first two or three times it will feel strange, and then it will become, à la Tony Robbins, a new norm, and your improvement will never stop. Some people would be embarrassed to tell colleagues that they read a book or went to a training, but if you flip that, you make it a strength. "Guys, I have been working on some communication skills, and I need your help. After each meeting, is it okay if I grab a minute with one of you? All I will ask is what you thought worked well and what could have been better." That statement flips the group from one whose mirror neurons pull you back into the old box to one that catapults you to a whole new level!

We have gone through this together, you and I, but we are not alone. The whole Own the Room community wants to hear how your latest presentation went. Post a note or photo or both on our Facebook page or follow me on Twitter at @billhoogterp. Visit www .owntheroom.com to access practice drills, watch videos, and learn about training events. You can download your own 30-day plan for even more rapid improvement and check off when you have played the drinking game, done voice modulations in real life, and more.

Public speaking is a metaphor for life. Getting up in front of an audience to deliver a brilliant and successful presentation can seem—like life itself—to be enormously complicated, requiring considerable reserves of talent, courage, personality, skill, and luck. Yet when it is reduced to its purest essence, it is quite simple. Be authentic. Get out of your own way. Connect. Make mistakes. Laugh. Be memorable. Attack life and squeeze it with big love.

Now you are the CEO of your own potential. Invest in yourself and your own growth. You are the brand, and today is your IPO.

Every tool that I have given you is meant to assist you along your own path up the mountain toward greatness. Reach for the three extra centimeters. Give yourself permission to be awesome, because you are.

Go. Be brilliant.

Index

About the Author

★

One of the most sought-after public speaking coaches in the world, Bill Hoogterp is the creator of Own the Room, a breakthrough methodology that helps busy professionals dramatically improve their public speaking skills in a very short period of time. From CEOs to celebrities, from German engineers to Hollywood agents, Bill and his team of world-class coaches have trained executives and professionals from various companies and industries on five continents. Own the Room is offered in multiple languages and includes training in related communication topics, leadership, and management.

For more information, please visit www.owntheroom.com or follow Bill on Twitter at @billhoogterp.